Teacup Tales

Folklore of the Hudson Valley

by

Pauline Hommell

Hope Farm Press & Bookshop

Saugerties New York

THIS PUBLICATION IS A

FACSIMILIE REPRINT

OF THE ORIGINAL BOOK

Published in 1958 by Vantage Press

1992

Hope Farm Press & Bookshop

7321 Rt 212 Saugerties NY 12477

made in U.S.A.   ISBN #0-910746-99-0

TEACUP TALES

Folklore of the Hudson Valley

by

PAULINE HOMMELL

Did you know that New York State had its own "Paul Revere"? She was a teenager who rode a thunderhoofed black horse through the midnight silence of Dutchess and Putnam Counties on April 25, 1777, pausing only long enough at each farm and tavern to cry: "Get up! Pa says to come....There's going to be a fight!"

The advancing British had burned Danbury, and young Sibyl Ludington, "Colonel Ludington's girl," had taken off from Carmel to spread the alarm while her father set about organizing the militia. What happened to Sibyl later is told in this facinating book, which re-creates many a scene from the Hudson Valley's wealth of lore.

Based upon fact, these tales relate events historic, heroic, tragic, humorous-and often, mysterious...for the Hudson is a valley where dwell ghosts still visible to those whose eyes are not "holden" so that they cannot see. Taken from Dutch, Revolutionary, Civil War, and other periods, these stories, in some instances, may have become distorted with the passage of years, but the basis of each is truth.

There are unsolved murders; a face at a window; a lonely

man who loved Jenny Lind to his dying day; a bachelor who married a baby; an eerie incident at Wiltwyck (Kingston), when the colonists' sentries vanished forever: the Black Rider who silently joined honest James Margison on a dark road in Mongaup Valley, between the rivers Mongaup and Neversink....

Pauline Hommell spent ten years sorting and writing these tales...and she has imbued the telling with that indefinable, all-pervasive spell which the Hudson and its valley cast upon those who know them well.

Reading Teacup Tales, you will sense the shadowy presence of Captain Kidd; of Peggy Shippen, wife to Benedict Arnold; of the tragic Cat Woman of Saugerties; and you may hear echos of the cry "Have you seen Sally Hamilton?" --the cry that led to the discovery of the body of a pretty maiden in a gray linsey gown and blue sunbonnet, brutally slain, on the bank of Murderer's Creek . . . a cry still ringing to haunt the ears of her slayer, be he man or shade . . . for in all the years he never has been found.

A collection of true Americana, rich in fact, in legend, and in atmosphere.

(from the dust jacket of the original edition)

To Iza
whose unfailing faith
gave me the courage
to write this
book

Foreword

PAULINE HOMMELL has woven a colorful fabric out of the many skeins of narrative which make up the folk heritage of the old Hudson River town of Saugerties. Like all good local historians, she has patiently listened to old-timers, read old books, consulted old manuscripts. She has a simple, straightforward way with a story and the people of her town will be proud of her handling of the tales that they have loved through the generations. Her title, moreover, is a good one for it implies just the sort of informality of style which the material demanded and received.

This is a significant contribution to the local history of the Hudson Valley. It unquestionably takes a place in the overall picture which will have been completed when each local historian of the state has given us a book as good as this one about the community in which he lives.

Octagon House CARL CARMER
Irvington-on-Hudson
New York

An Acknowledgment

In order to write this little volume it was necessary to seek the aid of many people. An author who attempts a book of folklore needs to question carefully the people of the locality about which the book is written. I have gone to one and another, asking, "When did this happen? Who was that person? When did this man live? What did that woman do to have her remembered all these years?"

And always people have been unfailingly kind, eager to help, anxious to tell me something that they thought might be of interest or help to me. Many have sought me out, thinking I might be able to use some little anecdote or incident. To those unnamed here I still offer a thankful meed of praise.

I had the extreme good fortune to be born beneath the shadow of the Catskills, in the valley of Hudson's Great River. My parents were steeped in the lore of the Low Dutchers. They told me many a yarn before I was grown. I gained from them an appreciation of the beauty of these majestic hills and mighty waters. It was they who instilled in me a reverence for the Past as well as a glowing hope for the Future. To their memory I give grateful tribute.

Among the people of Saugerties who have aided me in various and differing ways are: Mrs. Richard R. Keator, Dr. and Mrs. Lester A. Sonking, George de Mare, author of *The Empire,* Mr. and Mrs. William F. Russell, and the late Edmund Burhans.

I have also to thank Mrs Geraldine Cunningham and Mrs. Floyd Miller of Beacon, New York, Dr. Harold Thompson of Cornell University, author of *Body, Boots and Britches,* Carl Carmer, author of *The Hudson,* Miss Mabel Winter of Hempstead, New York, Mrs. C. M. Wynkoop of Kerhonkson New York, and Miss Ann Domidion of New York City.

CONTENTS

Foreword by CARL CARMER

The Cat Woman	9
The Bachelor Who Married the Baby	14
Murderer's Creek	16
The Big Blizzard	24
A Day to Remember	26
The Black Rider	30
The Face at the Window	32
Madam Brett's Garden	38
What Became of the Sentry?	41
Fulton's Folly and Mrs. Brink's Bonnet	43
Uncle Hans	46
Burgoyne's Ride	47
The Minister	50
"Boots" Van Steenburgh	52
Cornplanter Abeel	56
The Tale of the Murdered Slave Girl	60
A Pin in Her What?	62
The Forgotten Gravestone	64
Civil War Tales	67
The Story of Night John	71
The White Lady	72
Benedict Arnold's Wife	75
The Stone in the Wall	82
"A Voice in the Darkness"	84
The Story of the Little Sawyer	90

Prologue

THE OLD order changeth. The past is vanishing more swiftly and completely than it ever has in any era since the world began. Much that was unsatisfactory and evil has been replaced by the more satisfactory and the good. But, in going, the past has taken something with it—some indefinable element of peace and security that our present day lacks. And many of us look back with nostalgia to the quiet day, to the Victorian scene, and the early American times: the days of our forebears when life was simple.

The old town of Saugerties has stepped up into the marching ranks with the rest of the world. Big business has taken over—the Thruway is fast doing away with time and space; there's a new car in every garage; a TV in every home; the Central School and the Supermarket have replaced the little red schoolhouse and the corner grocery. And all this is good, but there is something lacking that is gone forever.

In this book I have tried to find that lost element, to recapture and assemble bits of the past and to construct them into something that will stand as a symbol of our lost years—not for this town alone, but for all the little towns in this broad land.

Teacup Tales
Folklore of the Hudson Valley

The Cat Woman

LET'S SEE. It must be nearly fifty years ago that she died, poor old thing. Before that she was a familiar sight on the streets, the cats following her as the rats did the Pied Piper of Hamelin. The harmless old creature was so sinister looking that if she had lived in Puritan days she would have been burned as a witch. Tall, thin, hollow-eyed, with a skin so dark that she might have almost been taken for a Negro, she slunk about the streets all hours of day and night, always with her feline following.

The attraction was a bag of fish scraps which she carried. The cats smelled it and they came running. Starved alley cats would follow poor old Ann for blocks. And to think that at last she had none but cats for company—nobody to speed her soul but the poor animals that she had befriended in their extremity. Who knows? Maybe they comforted her in her last hours, as human beings could never have done. Perhaps it is sacrilegious, but I like to think they are with her now.

To go on with the story, fact and fiction: Ann Taylor was born of good people and was well educated. When her father died and her mother remarried she came to Saugerties to live with her mother and stepfather. Her stepfather, Mr. Whittenden, was a man of considerable wealth, a professional man, and Ann had a life of ease and comfort. Always, even as a young girl, she was tall, angular, and dark. Also, she had a disconcerting way of talking about the affairs of the day in such a learned way that the few young men who approached her were hopelessly outdistanced in the mental field, and fled in dismay. Those were the days when girls were not supposed to know anything outside the realm of personal adornment and domestic problems. In vain her mother besought her to be more "maidenly." Ann was simply bewildered. She had merely tried to have an intelligent conversation with a man and he had not been interested.

Matters continued like this for several years. Ann was shunned by the men of the community. She was fast approaching thirty, an age, in those days, when a woman was labeled "old maid." Her mother had long since given up the struggle.

Then, suddenly, a man came to town and started the practice of law. He was a tall personable fellow, clever and affable, Robert Scott, by name. He seemed to have ample means for he lived in a fine house with servants to do his slightest bidding. All the mothers of eligible daughters strained and strove for his attention, but to most he seemed to be very cool and indifferent. It is true that he paid attention to many of the village maidens, but it looked as if he had no favorite among those who sought his attention.

Ann's stepfather was a business colleague, and often the young lawyer was invited to the Whittenden home for dinner. Soon the neighbors noticed that the two young people were often seen together and many a word was passed over the back fences. Great was the marveling. To think that poor Ann with her odd ways, her homely face, and her gawky figure had snared the most eligible man in town! Naught could come of it, said the neighbors. The handsome young lawyer would soon tire of poor, old, homely Ann.

However, sometimes the wisest and most observant are mistaken. On a balmy April morning Ann was seen walking down the street, clad in her usual nondescript garb, followed as ever by all the stray cats of the village. On her scrawny left hand blazed a magnificent diamond, and in her eyes was such a gleam of glory that "all who ran might read." Her lover had spoken. Ann, the unwanted, was wanted at last! And by the most sought-after man of the village.

The air was rife with rumors. They were to be married at once and sail for Europe. The groom's house was to be done over, many of the rooms in cloth of gold! The wedding was to be so magnificent that florists and caterers were to be sent for—'way off to New York, a hundred miles away! The bridal gown was to be made of satin so stiff that it could actually stand alone!

Meanwhile, the persons most intimately concerned went their ways calmly. Only the radiance in Ann's eyes and the glittering diamond on her hand bore mute testimony to the truth of the story that she was indeed betrothed. Months passed by. The young lawyer continued his occasional visits to the home of his bride-to-be. Frequently they were seen in each other's company.

Yet no word went abroad of the approaching nuptials. People began to whisper behind their hands. When was Ann to be married? Was she *ever* to be married? Perhaps it was all a trick on the part of the poor old maid to delude people for a time with the idea that she was going to marry the handsome young lawyer. Suspicious glances were cast at Ann and sneering remarks were made.

Then something happened to put everything else completely out of people's minds. Robert Scott disappeared. One night he said a casual good-by to his secretary, left his office, and stepped out into the sleety storm (for it was late November). He was never seen in Saugerties again. He left a thriving and lucrative practice and many loyal and faithful friends. These all stoutly maintained that he must have met with foul play, although no evidence confirming this statement could be discovered. Everything in his office and his business was in excellent order. No reason for suicide could be advanced. Many, in fact most, of the townfolk, said derisively that he had merely grown tired of his bargain with the queer old maid, and had simply "walked out on her," "given her the mitten," as the saying was in those days.

No stone was left unturned to find his whereabouts, but all to no avail. Finally the searchers gave up the quest, and the town settled down to its regular routine. But this was after many months of diligent and careful combing of the countryside. The search had been carried to far distant cities, but not the slightest trace of Scott had been found. It was finally conceded that he must have taken his life, but where and how?

Meanwhile, Ann went about the streets as usual with her bag of fish scraps. Nobody dared venture to speak to her about Scott; her gaze was so fixed and fierce, and her bearing so aloof. Only to the cats was she gentle and compassionate.

Suddenly her stepfather died. Then came to light the startling fact that the man, who had posed as powerfully wealthy for so many years, was practically bankrupt. Even the home had to be sold to pay his debts. The cynics nodded their heads sagely. No wonder Robert Scott had vanished so suddenly. Probably he had discovered that his future father-in-law was practically penniless, and, as rats desert a sinking ship, he had left Ann. Well, the old maid would have to get down from her high horse now and do a bit of good, honest work. Maybe she might even quit carrying fish scraps around town.

But there were those who pitied the friendless creature and wished they might do something to help her. She was alone now, her mother having died several years before. However, nobody was brave enough to approach her with an offer to help. Ann took the few belongings which were hers, and moved out of the imposing mansion which had been her home for so many, long years. Her scanty means made it possible for her to rent a small house in the very poorest section of the village, down near the river. The view was magnificent, but the poor shanty had a leaking roof and the wind whistled through every crack and crevice, and there seemed to be millions of them. With Ann went her cats, all twelve of them; and when one blustery night, many years after her misfortune, a strange, gaunt, black cat crouched on her window sill, the friendless old woman quickly opened the window and let him in. Those were days when food was cheap and fish scraps could be had for the asking, otherwise, the almost penniless, old gentlewoman could never have cared for her charges.

The black cat waxed sleek and glossy. His amber eyes often sought Ann's in almost human inquiry. Many a conversation they had together beside the rusty kitchen stove. The other cats were merely loved pets. Black Bob was a loving and beloved friend.

But as the years went on, poor Ann found it harder and harder to keep soul and body together. She tramped the streets, seeking the cheapest foods to be found. And every night there was the heavy bag of fish scraps to carry home, along with her few meager parcels. She grew thinner and weaker with the passage of time, as her feline family grew huskier and more beautiful.

One dour evening in November, just twenty years after Robert Scott had so mysteriously disappeared, old Ann wearily entered her hovel to find Black Bob eagerly waiting for her in her one-and-only rocker with its gay plaid cushion that Ann had left drawn up before the old kitchen stove. Bob leaped down when she entered. The woman sank exhausted into the chair. The cat fawned about her feet, but Ann was too exhausted to notice.

Suddenly a voice spoke out of the deepening gloom—a voice she had not heard in twenty years. "Ann," it said softly.

Ann lifted her head, but it seemed strangely heavy. She raised her weary eyelids with difficulty. It seemed to her bemused senses that a tall man was standing beside her knee where the black cat had been purring a moment before.

"Robert," she whispered faintly, and with that faint whisper her head fell back, her eyes opened and stared sightlessly at the ceiling. A long shudder shook her thin body. She lay suddenly very still.

So the neighbors found her—sitting before her cold hearth, the cats clamoring about her, the packages dropped from her lifeless hands.

"Well," said Mrs. Wolven to Mrs. Schoonmaker, who had come to "sit up," "somebody has got to put all these varmints out of the way. But where in time is that 'Black Bob,' as she called him? He was always at her heels, and now, drat him, he can't be found."

Nor was Black Bob ever found. The neighbors concluded that he must have followed Ann on that last day of her weary wandering, and failed to return. "Good riddance," they grumbled, "one less to dump into the river."

Could Black Bob have been Robert Scott? Could a human being come back to earth in the form of an animal? There are many who will answer those questions in the affirmative. But be that as it may. Everyone is entitled to his own opinion. This is a folklore story, not a treatise on the transmigration of souls, and it is comforting to author and readers alike to think that Ann and her beloved walk the streets of the City of Peace hand in hand. And who knows? Perhaps the cats scamper gaily along beside them.

The Bachelor Who Married the Baby

IN A little Dutch village not far from here there was born in the year 1750, to Hanse and Katerina Homel, a boy whom they named Petrus. Petrus was a sturdy youngster (as of necessity all who survived those hard days must have been) and he grew and thrived. He worked hard and played hard, though there was little time for much of the latter. As soon as a boy was old enough to hold shovel, hoe, or ax, he was hustled out of his mother's arms and into a life of unremitting toil. And Petrus was no exception. In the few spare moments which were his, he loved to read the Dutch books which made up his mother's scanty library, and then to discuss them with his friend, Samuel Freelich, whose German parents lived not far from Petrus' home. Samuel was a fair-haired, ruddy-faced boy inclined toward stoutness, while Petrus, like his father, was lean and dark and sinewy. Between these two boys, so different in physical aspect, there existed a friendship which was as warm as it was lasting.

Where Petrus was, there you would find Samuel; and wherever Samuel went, there, if it were humanly possible, also went Petrus.

Growing up together side by side, these two Dutch and German American boys heard the call of their country in the early days of the Revolution. Petrus and Samuel were among the first to offer their services, were accepted, and marched away. But before they left, Petrus had whispered a vital question into the rosy ear of shy, little Rachel, a neighbor lassie, whose downcast eyes and blushing cheeks quite plainly told the dark-eyed, slow-speaking Petrus that he had much to hope for should the will of Providence be that he return one day from the battlefront.

Petrus and Samuel acquitted themselves well, fought through skirmishes and battles (at least one of which is now famous in military history), came through unscathed, and marched home, footsore, older in years and experience, but comrades as they had always been.

Petrus married his fair-haired Rachel and settled down comfortably on the farm whose broad acres his own unstinted toil had helped to wrest from the wilderness, while Samuel went home to his father's house and labored cheerfully on the rolling hills which would some day be his. Still friends and companions, the two young men found time to spend hours in each other's society, and Samuel was always a welcome visitor at the stone house in the valley where the comely Rachel presided over the domestic affairs of friend Petrus.

One day news came to Samuel on his hill farm that a little stranger had arrived at the house in the valley. At his earliest convenience, Samuel hurried down the hill to greet the newest member of the house of Homel.

Petrus had long worried over his friend's unmarried state and had often chided him for not following his own excellent example of taking a buxom bride and settling down. So, on this lovely day in June, 1783, as Petrus held his infant daughter in his arms, he remarked jocosely, "Here is a wife for you, Samuel. All you need to do is to have patience for a few years, and when she is grown there is no man on the face of this earth to whom I would surrender her more willingly."

Now, right here comes the proof of the old adage: "Truth is stranger than fiction." The years passed and in time little Annetje grew into as lovely a girl as her mother had been when young Petrus had marched off to the war. And who should come a-wooing her but Samuel! Not that he was the only one — far from it! But strange to say he was the most favored among her many swains. Turning away from the youths who sought her hand, Annetje gave her love to sober Samuel, her father's friend, the faithful warden of her baby days. One fine day there was a wedding in the stone church in Katsbaan, and it was Annetje who rode happily off, after the ceremony, on the pillion behind her husband, Samuel, her arms reaching fondly around his thick waist, her glowing, rosy cheek on his shoulder.

And that ends the story. As far as I know they lived happily ever after. Our family chronicle says nothing to the contrary. But I have always been deeply interested in this sweet, old-time romance. Annetje made a good, true, and loving wife, and I firmly believe, and as far as tradition knows, Samuel, the indifferent, was her adoring husband to the end of their days.

Murderer's Creek

IT WAS drawing near to evening. The day had been hot and sultry. The breeze which blew through the open window from over the Hudson was refreshingly cool. Sally straightened her aching back. She was ladling apple butter, made that day from the early Pound Sweets, from the big black kettle into a stone crock.

Her sister, Taney, was making *supaan*. "It's a light supper and Dan'l always likes it," she said. "Will you run down cellar, Sally, and get a pitcher of buttermilk?"

The two women were working in the "back" kitchen of a small stone dwelling house standing on a hill above the Hudson River in the Village of Athens. The time was late July, 1813. Sally had come down from her parents' home in the upper village early that morning to help her sister "put up" preserves. The times were hard, and every bit of food must be conserved. Since the outbreak of war, over a year ago, many able-bodied men had enlisted. As yet, Sally's brother-in-law had listened to his wife's pleas. But he might go at any time, and hungry mouths must be fed.

As they ate the simple supper of *supaan*, molasses, and buttermilk, Sally thought yearningly of the bright-flowered calico Pa had bought for her last week in Catskill. It had a background of dark green leaves with tiny bright red flowers sprinkled over it. Ma was going to help her start it tomorrow. She rose. "I'll help wash up, Taney, and then I'll be going. I want to get home to help Ma with the last of the butter before dark."

There had been more work to do than Sally had reckoned. It was nearly eight o'clock. She hoped Ma wouldn't be worried or mad. She *was* tired. The night had turned cool after the sunset. Sally went up the lane from her sister's house and turned into the main road by the old Van Loon dwelling. That house and many others were already dark. There was naught to keep a tired body out of bed after nightfall in the little river village a century and a half ago. It was pleasant and peaceful to walk along the board sidewalks or in the tall grass beside the road, alone in the darkness. A yellow moon was drifting in and out of cloud banks. There was a group of people talking on the corner by the church. The supper! Sally had forgotten. Mrs. Van Schaack and Mrs. Van Loon were waiting for her.

"Where've you been so late, Sally? Down to Taney's?

How's the baby? Ain't sick, is he? Bad weather for babies and this his second summer, too."

The women joined Sally, and the three walked along together, the women chattering about the supper and what they had "taken in." "Your Ma's apple pie was good, Sally. Oh, you made it? Well, the man that gets you will be a lucky one."

At the store of Abram Van Hoeson there were joyful cries: "Hello, Sally, come on in. We've got to buy some groceries. Pa got home late. Nothing to eat home but garden stuff."

Eliza and Dan'l Hallenbeck, friends of Sally's, urged her to go in with them.

"I've been away all day. I must get back," she told them.

Sally left the young folks and the two older women and started up the hill.

Mrs. Hamilton looked up from her knitting. "Well, it's about time you was comin'" she said. "Oh, it's you, Taney? Wherever is Sally? I've been wonderin' all day what kept her. She shouldn't a stayed overnight. I told her and she promised to be back last night. Pa and I waited up till nearly ten. She did? Well, she ain't come. When did she leave? No. I tell you, she never did come."

Mrs. Hamilton tied on her sunbonnet. "I'm goin' right out to look. Somethin's wrong. Sally never did stay out anywhere all night without tellin' us. You take the baby and run over to the Bogardus's, Taney. Tell Fred to go down the river road and I'll go up the hill."

Fred Bogardus tipped back his hat and scratched his head. "They ain't nothin' could a happened to her, Taney. She's a grown woman. They ain't been no strangers in town, and nobody around these parts would molest a body. Ain't there some place she could a stayed? Yeah, I'll take Joe Haynes with me."

The two men started out. They walked leisurely down the hill together. Nobody was really concerned yet. The two men figured that Sally had been induced by some friend or neighbor to stay overnight (perhaps sickness in the family had caused them to ask her). They would stop along the road and inquire.

"Ye seen anything of Sally Hamilton? She didn't come home last night. No, it ain't anything like that," said Fred angrily, "and don't go insinuatin' things. Sally's as good a girl as ever drew the breath of life. Yes, she did. No, she didn't."

At Van Hoeson's store they had the first clue. "Ye did? When? And she went on? Which way?"

"How should I know?" said Van Hoeson, testily. "I was weighing out flour and I'm a busy man. I don't stop to watch folks up and down the road. I suppose she turned the corner and went up to her folks." He pulled down a string of dried onions and cut off four. He weighed them and handed them over to Anson Schuyler. He measured some snuff and put it in a paper.

"Who's missing?" asked Schuyler. "Why, she was down to Taney's yesterday. I saw her there."

"Well, she ain't there now," said Fred, shortly, and went out.

Meanwhile, Mrs. Hamilton had stopped at every house. "Hev ye seen Sally? No, she was down to Taney's all day. No, she didn't come home. We waited up last night, but we didn't worry. We thought the girls had worked late and she decided to stay overnight. Yes, she did leave there about eight o'clock last night, but she never did come home."

By this time Mrs. Hamilton was wiping her eyes on her apron. "I jest can't help but think something must have happened to her. No, I know they ain't been anybody strange in town. But then it's not like Sally to stay out and not tell us. No, I know there's something wrong."

At the Hallenbeck home she had the first inkling of disaster. Dan'l was out helping his father, but Eliza was there. "Why, we seen Sally last night. We wanted her to come to the store with us, but she said she had to get home to help you with the last of the butter, Mrs. Hamilton. She left us. I thought she went on up the hill."

Meanwhile, Fred Bogardus and Joe Haynes had pursued their inquiry. From door to door traveled the query: "Have you seen Sally Hamilton?"

"Have you seen Sally Hamilton?"

Over the entire village, both upper and lower portions, the anguished question went ringing, and always the answer was "No."

Mrs. Van Loon and Mrs. Van Schaack told of walking as far as the store with her. They told of the conversation, of how Sally had been anxious to get home—of how she had been her usual light-hearted self—of how she had left them. Yes, they *thought* she had turned up the hill. No, they were not certain. They thought she had.

"Have you seen Sally Hamilton?"

There was widespread alarm. By six o'clock of that pleasant July afternoon the entire community was alerted. Sally Hamilton was missing. She had left her home at an early hour of the preceding day and had not returned. Searching parties were formed. The Sheriff from Catskill, the county seat, came, bringing with him an organized posse. The girl's description was carefully recorded: five feet four inches tall, light-brown curls, hazel eyes, weight about 140 pounds, wearing a gray linsey dress and blue sunbonnet. Very white teeth, pleasant smile—small mole beside her left eyebrow.

"Have you seen Sally Hamilton?"

Great was the anxiety and many the conjectures. Sally was well beloved by all. She was a "good" girl, as Fred Bogardus had said. If anything had happened to her, if anyone had enticed her, it must have been by some trick. She would never have gone willingly.

Samuel Hamilton was a calm man, not easily moved, but

the disappearance of his beloved daughter was like a crushing blow on the head. At first he had sat stunned—then he had arisen and joined one of the searching posses. He had not returned. Mrs. Hamilton sat by the window of the cottage dry-eyed, clutching in her hands Sally's red apron, clinging to it as if the inanimate cloth were a bit of the girl she had borne and raised. The sun sank nearer the horizon.

"Have you seen Sally Hamilton?"

Pete Murdock and Tunis Ryer, two of the men of the Catskill posse, were tramping along the banks of the little stream which, nameless, flowed through the village of Athens, dividing it into two sections, the upper village and the lower village. They, with two others, had crossed the bridge, a plank of which was missing. The two others had gone upstream, and Tunis and Pete were working down toward the river, one on each bank of the creek. The men who had crossed with them were Athens men, and they noted idly that a plank of the bridge was gone. Someone, some time recently, had pulled out one of the planks. But why? They were too concerned with the matter of Sally Hamilton to speculate. Each pair went its own way.

Suddenly Tunis Ryer gave a great shout: "Pete, I've found her!"

Pete Murdock waded the little stream (ever after known as Murderer's Creek) and joined his companion on the north bank. Sally Hamilton lay on her back, gazing sightlessly into the eyes of her horrified finders. The skirts of her gray linsey dress were wrapped around her. Her arms were wide-flung amid the weeds of the creekside. Her brown curls lay fanwise around her head, the side of which had been crushed by a terrific blow. There was a dark bruise on her cheek, and blood had stained one side of her face beyond recognition.

It needed but one startled glance from the men to tell them that life had long since left the body at their feet.

Now, they had one dreadful task to accomplish. Theirs was the duty to tell the community that they "had seen Sally Hamilton!"

"I tell ye: I did it. I saw her walkin' along that night and I went up to her and I says, 'Sally Hamilton, I'm agoin' to kill ye,' and I took a club which I was a-carryin' and I smashed her head in."

The speaker was Cavanaugh, a small, grotesque figure of a man. He was clad in nondescript garments and carried an old rifle of Revolutionary War vintage.

He had come to the office of the Athens village clerk, Isaac Northrup, and told that dignitary that he wanted to "confess." The time was late August, 1813, a few weeks after the tragic death of the young and lovely Sally.

Mr. Northrup looked suspiciously at Cavanaugh. "How did you happen to be hanging around so late that night, Pat?" he asked gently.

"'Twan't late—'twas only jest dark, and I'd no place to sleep that night. I was aimin' to stay up all night anyhow. I made up my mind I was agoin' to kill somebody. The world done me awful wrong always. I had to take it out on somebody, and Sally Hamilton was just as good as any."

Northrup glanced at the Sheriff, who was listening to the story also. The two men, good friends, had been chewing tobacco and talking in Northrup's office when Cavanaugh had come in with his confession.

The Sheriff winked at Northrup. "Well, never mind now, Pat," he said. "You go along and we'll arrest you tomorrow."

"But I'm supposed to hang—I tell you!" shouted Pat. "I killed an innocent young girl! I'm dangerous! Lock me up!"

With difficulty the men persuaded the would-be murderer to get on his way. After they'd bolted the door behind his protesting figure the Sheriff turned to Northrup.

"Ike, the poor fool is battier than a loon. He was locked

up in our own jail in Catskill since early June and was released only a week ago Tuesday. He couldn't kill anything except flies on the night of July 28th, and, by jing—he could probably kill plenty of them. The jail is full. Awful delinquent flies we got in Catskill."

The Sheriff chuckled, and then sobered instantly. "No clues as yet, Northrup? Nothing at all to go on? Strange."

The man was tall and thin, with a sharp, foxlike face. He looked at the Sheriff boldly. "Yes, I did," he said sullenly. "I couldn't help it. He was bigger than me. He attacked her and then when she fought and screamed he hit her with the bridge plank he'd picked up as we came along. No, no, I didn't hit her. I was carryin' the plank, as I told you before, and I laid it down when Sickledge found the girl. Do I git the money? A thousand dollars, ain't it? No, I never had nothing to do with it. I was just with Sickledge when he done it."

This monologue had gone on for hours in the office of the Sheriff of Greene County. The man had appeared fully two years after the tragic death of Sally to say that he knew who had done the deed. Now, he was wishing he were a thousand miles away. There were many pointed questions, and several that he could not answer satisfactorily. If only he hadn't thought of this way of "getting even" with Sickledge and making a nice boodle at the same time!

The Sheriff was skeptical. There was a false ring to the man's words. Often the Sheriff tripped the man, and he contradicted flatly what he had said before.

"Where is Sickledge?" asked the Sheriff. Lant knew and could lead the Sheriff and his men to the culprit. Why hadn't he come forward with all this information before? He was afraid, Lant confessed. The Sheriff acknowledged grimly that there was cause for fear.

With Lant under arrest, they took him protesting loudly to Sickledge's hideout. They returned to Catskill with both rascals, but the Sheriff was far from satisfied. The men told stories which were very unsatisfactory as far as pinning the crime on either was concerned.

Court was convened and both gave testimony. The truth, after much astute questioning by one of the best lawyers of the day, was finally brought out. Sickledge was innocent. He was proven so by an ironclad alibi. On the night of the murder he had been in a tavern in Cairo, several miles from Athens, and had been there from early evening until the tavern closed after midnight. He and Lant had had a fight subsequently. He had administered a terrible beating and Lant had sworn to "get even."

The latter was convicted of perjury, sentenced and imprisoned. Sickledge went on his way. Another half-opened door to the solution of the murder of Sally Hamilton had slammed in the faces of the investigators.

So today, in the year of our Lord one thousand nine hundred and fifty-eight, the people of the quiet village of Athens go back and forth on their workaday errands from the Upper Village to the Lower Village which is Athens proper. Sally and her parents and her sister and her family sleep in the "old" cemetery on the hill. Somewhere in the world the murderer has long since slept his last sleep, too. But one wonders on a quiet, moon-brightened midnight in late July, if a lass with brown curls and bright hazel eyes, dressed neatly in the garb of a long-gone day, doesn't stand for a time by the wooden rail of the bridge over "Murderer's Creek."

The Big Blizzard

It was sort of fun—for the young folks, I mean, not the adults. (It was grim labor, suffering, and death for many.) It started on Sunday night. It snowed all that night, Monday, and Monday night, all day Tuesday and Tuesday night.

The wind blew most of the time. When people started to dig out on Wednesday, they found the snow blown in such great heaps that in many cases they had to make tunnels through the snow. It was too deep to be shoveled out entirely. Remember, in those days, they had no motor-driven snowplows.

Many funny things, as well as terrible things, happened in that great storm. Edmund Burhans, who lived to be four-score-and-ten, told one of the funniest stories of the great storm. He related that after the second day of shoveling, the snow had begun to alternately melt and freeze. This made the sidewalks and streets extremely icy and dangerous.

Eddie was making his way carefully down the steep slope of Partition Street, which in those days was not graded as it is today and consequently much more precipitous. A scuffling sound behind him warned him that something or somebody was about to crash into him. He jumped, but not soon enough! A huge, six-foot giant, weighing well over two hundred pounds, landed squarely upon him. Mr. Burhans, who was short and thin, was all but crushed beneath the larger man's bulk. Always thoughtful of others, Eddie struggled out from under the tremendous weight and inquired anxiously, "Are you hurt?"

"Not a bit," said the big man jovially. "I've had four falls this morning and this is the best fall I've had yet."

My mother's mother, Grandmother Margison, lived in a cottage belonging to Mother on Mother's estate, at the time of the blizzard. Her son, Uncle Cyrus, lived with his mother and was manager of my mother's farm, for my mother was a widow. The cottage was down below the hill, and to get to the farm buildings my uncle had to make his way up the slope, against the furious blasts of wind and snow which buffeted him unmercifully. To insure his finding his way back, he fastened a long, stout rope around a porch pillar of the cottage, and the other end about his waist. Then he started forth.

Grandmother, filled with anxiety and dire misgivings, climbed hastily to the attic as soon as Uncle Cyrus started forth. (I forgot to say that the storm spread a peculiar darkness over the earth, and through the hours of broad daylight a strange, dark haze brooded over the land.) Grandmother Margison's intentions were to watch her son's progress up the hill, through the small attic window. Arriving at the top of the steps, she groped her way across the floor to the tiny window and peered fearfully out. Nothing but black, impenetrable darkness fell upon her startled eyes. Grandmother shaded her eyes with her hand and pressed her face closer to the window. Her eyes could not pierce the blackness. Where was her son in that awful, murky gloom? She moaned aloud and wrung her hands in helpless agony.

"Why, Ma, what are you doing over there looking into the chimney hole?" said a startled voice behind her. The light of a kerosene lamp in the hands of her daughter, Aunt Nell, faintly illuminated the inky blackness of the attic.

With a gasp of relief my grandmother turned from her post of vigil, and sought out the small window from whence she could see something of the storm. In her haste to see the fury of the blizzard, she had made her way to the chimney, mistaking it for the window, and when found by Aunt Nell, had been staring fixedly at the bricks of the chimney.

A Day to Remember

It was the morning of July 4th, 1897. Mamma stirred sleepily. She supposed she would have to get up very soon. There was a big day ahead: A chicken dinner with all the fixin's to prepare; ice cream and cake to make; vegetables to gather; the baby to look after; the children to watch so they wouldn't blow their heads off with the giant "crackers" that Papa insisted on buying every Fourth. And besides those, he had to have torpedoes, sparklers, Roman candles, sky rockets, set pieces, etc. So much money for nothing, Mamma thought.

A concussion that shook the house broke in upon her gloomy reverie. "Glory, what are they up to?" she moaned as she rushed to the window. Charlie, Maggie, and Annie were all giggling excitedly at a safe distance and the "cracker" was still smoking under the window.

"Now, don't you children set off another one of those contraptions until Papa comes down from milking, or I'll take them all away from you," scolded Mamma. "You woke up the baby and I was hoping she'd sleep awhile yet."

Mamma hurried into her clothes and went downstairs to prepare breakfast after first caring for baby who was very damp and very cranky.

After breakfast the serious preparation for the Big Day started. Papa was to kill a good-sized chicken—the children were to wash the dishes, and she, Mamma, would make the ice cream.

Several neighbors would be in after supper to watch the fireworks and there must be ice cream and cake to serve.

The custard for the cream was put on the range to cook, and Mamma went down the hill to the garden for vegetables. On returning to the house a scorching smell struck her fairly in the face with a great blast. The ice cream! Mamma ran! It was too late. The cream was scorched beyond hope. The only thing to do was to throw it into the swill pail for the pigs. And there it went. Where had they been, queried Mamma, indignantly. Nowhere, they said innocently. They had been right here. They hadn't noticed any smell.

A second kettle, full of custard, was put on to cook and Mamma went to work on the chicken. The rooster was plump and young and looked like a good dinner. Mamma decided she would make dumplings. But what was that large fatty lump under the bird's wing? It was something alien to any chicken she had ever dressed. "I'll not cook a chicken with anything like that in him," said Mamma firmly. So Papa had perforce to kill another.

Meanwhile, the second kettle, full of ice cream, had begun to scorch. Mamma snatched it off the fire, dumped the contents of the kettle quickly into another receptacle and fervently hoping the "scorch" would not taste.

She hastily stirred up a cake and put it in the oven and proceeded to scald, pluck, and dress the second chicken. Lo and behold—the second chicken had an identical lump. Not for Mamma! Into the kettle he went with the other to be cooked for the dog and cats.

But what now? What for dinner? An examination of the icebox disclosed some salt mackerel. "Well, we will have mackerel," said Mamma calmly.

"Mamma, the cake!" screamed twelve-year-old Annie. The cake was burned beyond the hope of salvage.

"I'll make another," said Mamma, with resignation and complete despair. "Maggie, go draw a bucket of water. This mackerel will have to be freshened, if we are to have any dinner today."

Down into the well went the bucket and Maggie started to pull slowly to bring it to the surface. The bump and splash were simultaneous—the bucket had gone peacefully to the bottom of the well—the rope broken!

With the second cake in the oven, the hired man, freezing the scorched ice cream, and Papa splicing the well rope, Mamma decided her vegetable garden trip had not been too successful. There must be some canned vegetables in the pantry. She poked around until a large can of factory-prepared corn came to light.

That would have to do for an extra vegetable. With a look at the ice cream to see if it was "there," Mamma opened the can of corn. What was that spidery, black thing among the creamy mass of kernels? Spidery! Spidery was the word. It was the body of an unfortunate insect which had met his doom in the succulent, thickened corn. Into the swill pail with the burned cake and cream went the corn.

"We'll just have to get along with green beans and potatoes for dinner. That and mackerel will have to do. You can't have dessert," said Mamma, icing the cake. "This and the cream are for tonight. Papa, will you *please* watch baby. She's playing on the floor there. I'm afraid she'll put something in her mouth that shouldn't go there. Put her on your desk. You can watch her for five minutes, can't you? I don't know where the girls and Charlie went."

"Sure, sure," said Papa soothingly. "Don't worry, Mary Ellen, everything will turn out all right. You'll see."

With that he lifted baby and placed her on his desk.

"Give her something to play with and keep hold of her if you're going to read," said Mamma nervously.

Papa complied. Mamma worked busily, preparing dinner and finishing up last preparations for the evening spread. A peaceful holiday quiet lay over the bright summer noontide.

Maybe Papa was right, mused Mamma. She *was* inclined to worry too much. But it had been such an exasperating day. One thing after another. And where could the children have gone? They'd said something about taking a walk to the creek. They'd had their orders. They all knew enough not to stick even their toes in. The creek was dangerous—full of quicksand and sudden deep holes. They would not go in. Mamma felt sure of that, but where could they have gone so long? Just then the sound of their voices reassured her. Good that Papa was around to watch the baby so she could work. She guessed she'd fry the mackerel now. The potatoes and beans were done. Too bad about the chickens. Well, it just couldn't be helped. She squeezed the mackerel dry and laid it in the hot fat. She would cut some of the late roses to put in a jar on the piazza. Sailes and Maxwells would all be here tonight. She would tell Papa to ask Tice, too. Poor old Tice! Living all alone in that gloomy, dreary, old house. He had so little, and she and Papa had so much. God had blest them so! They had the older children and their health, and now baby had come and she was so lovely, and never a bit of trouble. Yes, she would tell him right away before she forgot it.

"*Papa!*" A cry of an avenging angel shattered the calm of the peaceful day.

Papa jumped, as if one of his own giant crackers had exploded under him. "I've got her, Mama—she's all right," he shouted.

Mamma's voice was ominously quiet. "Yes, she's all right," she said, bitterly, as she brushed past her husband to the desk, "but you just didn't happen to notice, did you, that the entire contents of the ink bottle is in her lap."

The Black Rider

IN 1850 my great grandfather and his numerous sons were in the tanning business in Mongaup Valley, New York. The region around the Neversink and Mongaup Rivers abounded in hemlock trees. The bark of this tree contains a dye indispensable to the leather business of that day, so the hemlocks were ruthlessly destroyed so that the feet of our forebears could be properly shod.

Martin Margison and his sons labored indefatigably from early morning till late at night. Those were the days when people literally "earned their bread by the sweat of their brows." One day, James, one of the younger sons, mounted his horse and rode to a distant city on a business errand for his father. Coming home late that night, along a lonely road, the young man thought nervously of highwaymen, for he carried a good-sized roll of greenbacks, besides a bag of gold and silver in his pockets. When he was about five miles from home, on the dreariest and most forsaken stretch of the roadway, he was startled by a rider appearing suddenly beside him, having come apparently out of an abandoned road, which led, as far as James Margison knew, only to an old and forgotten slate quarry, and endless reaches of uninhabited cranberry marshes.

"Good evening, stranger," said James, with a heartiness which he did not feel. "Are you going far?"

The rider beside him made no answer to this cheery greeting. James Margison gave a quick, sidelong glance at the figure which had so abruptly and unaccountably joined him in this most desolate and lonesome bit of wasteland. The beast which the stranger was riding was the most beautiful bit of horseflesh my uncle had ever seen. Sixteen hands high, midnight black, with a mane which cascaded over his arching neck, and a tail which nearly touched the ground. The man who sat on his back was fashionably garbed, with the exception that, instead of the high-crowned beaver hat of the day, he wore a cap pulled low over his eyes, and with one gloved hand he held his shawl over the lower part of his face, so his features were practically obscured.

Once more my uncle assayed a bit of conversation: "Didn't know anyone lived on that bit of road from whence you came, my friend," he pursued genially.

On receiving no answer from the muffled figure beside him, blind terror seized Uncle Jim. He dug his heels into the flanks of his own exhausted horse, thinking somehow he might outdistance the silent rider. But his hopes were vain. The splendid animal beside him leaped as his horse leaped, and together they thundered down the gloomy roadway. James Margison's horse seemed as anxious to free himself from the black horse and his rider as James was. But finally exhaustion caused him to abate his speed. With effortless ease the other horse had kept directly abreast of him. And so they rode in silence over the midnight road until the straggling houses of the village of Mongaup Valley began to make their appearance.

"Surely, now," thought Uncle Jim, "he will drop behind."

But the strange horse and his strange rider went with James Margison right up to his brother's door. There, when Uncle Jim drew rein, the Black Rider did also. Uncle Jim pulled his feet out of the stirrups and dropped to the ground.

His exhausted horse cantered wearily off to the stable. Jim rushed to his brother's bedroom window "Peter, Peter," he called excitedly, "come out, come out, for the love of heaven."

Hearing his brother getting up, James Margison turned and glanced fearfully over his shoulder. The Black Horse and his rider had vanished — as if the earth had suddenly opened and swallowed them! There was no sight or sound of their sinister presence in the dark, silent night. His own horse, he discovered later, was cowering and trembling in its stall, but no trace of the great black stallion could be found. Peter Margison, my grandfather, was inclined at the time to chide his brother for being a foolish, imaginative boy who had perhaps been imbibing during his day in town.

But, the next morning, when James showed him in the soft mud the clear prints of the hoofs of two horses which had turned in the gate together, Peter Margison shook his head and turned pale. The prints of one horse's shoes continued on to the stable; the other prints, clear and distinct, and much smaller than those of Margison's horse, stopped squarely in the drive, right at the place where Uncle Jim had dismounted from his own horse and rushed so madly toward his brother's window.

The Face at the Window

IT WAS the spring of 1861. Sumter had been fired upon. The country was already in the throes of civil war—a war that, up to that time, was the greatest and most terrible conflict which had even been fought upon the face of the earth. So, if people seemed indifferent and cruel, they may have been just terribly preoccupied, terribly terrified. That is their only justification.

The jail physician turned away from the broken-down cot. "He's dead," he said indifferently. "Been dead eight . . . ten hours, I'd say."

The brilliant May sunshine streamed through the small-paned, dirty window of the jail and fell upon the ragged figure lying on the bed. The face was turned to the wall, and a look of peace overspread the haggard features. The form was that of a worn and shabby man, dirty beyond any powers of description. He might have been sixty-five or eighty-five. It was difficult to tell.

"Well, better get him out of here," said the jailer. "He belongs in Saugerties anyhow. Jack, go get an undertaker from there."

In a few hours, a long, black wagon stopped at the jail, and the silent form was roughly bundled up in an old canvas, carried out, and placed in the wagon; the horses' heads were turned toward Saugerties. The Saugerties Bard had started on his last earthly journey.

Henry Backus was born in a small Greene County Village some time toward the end of the eighteenth century. His parents were people of some considerable wealth, and his brother graduated from West Point and became a colonel in the regular army. He played a brilliant part in the Mexican War and was repeatedly cited for gallantry in action. Backus Senior had also been a colonel and had taken part in the War of 1812; he had been wounded in one of the battles on the Niagara frontier. The Bard, himself, took no part in the military affairs of the country but was a great lover of music, which tendency he had inherited from his father. He loved nature and the out-of-doors; he was wont to take his fiddle and his dogs and roam for days around the countryside.

It was May, 1820. All of Ulster County was beautiful, with the lush, green loveliness of the springtide. Saugerties, fast becoming a thriving community and soon to be incorporated as a village, was basking in the glory of that long-ago spring morning, when Henry Backus sauntered down Main Street, his dog at his heels. He was bound on an errand for his father, commissioned to go to the saddler's for the saddle trim the elder Backus had ordered; but Henry was in no hurry. His fife needed attention; so he was headed for the house of his friend, Cornelis Post, who was adept at repairing all kinds of musical instruments.

As Henry strolled up the pleasant, tree-shaded road, there was not a care on his mind. He was young, barely twenty-three, and had secured the position of teacher in the local school—five dollars a month and board. Besides, he had several pupils for musical instruction; fife, drum, and bugle. A man could prosper on that income in the 1820's. And Henry Backus didn't care much for material gain, anyway. Buying and selling, bartering and bickering, he looked upon with distaste and aversion. With the blue sky above him, a fiddle slung over his shoulder, a dog at his heels, and a hunch of bread and cheese in his pocket, what more could a man ask of life?

Just ahead of him on the path was a slight figure in a sprigged muslin dress. The high waistline was marked with a black velvet ribbon. Beneath the ruffled skirt peeped two small feet shod in black slippers, the straps of which crossed demurely over white stockings. A huge bonnet crowned shining black curls. The pink satin bows were tied under a round, cleft chin and black lace mitts covered the small hands.

That pleasant picture Henry observed as he came abreast of the modish little lady. His long, easy strides had brought him up to her, and he did not hurry to pass by.

At Cornelis Post's he asked casually whether there were any strangers in town. Cornelis laughed, "You've been seeing our neighbor's cousin, Alida Legg. Ach, but she is good to feast one's eyes on."

"I haven't exactly been feasting my eyes," Henry said stiffly, "but I could not help seeing her when I passed her down the road a piece."

"Well, I'll see that you meet her. She is truly a *lievelich vrouw*," said Cornelis carelessly.

So in due time Henry met Alida Legg. She proved to be all that his first glimpse of her had suggested. The young couple had many a pleasant stroll together, for Alida loved the beauties of earth as much as Henry did. Being an orphan, she was not so strictly chaperoned as most of the girls of her time; so the young people were together much more than was the custom in those days when girls were kept constantly under the maternal eye. Occasionally, Henry wheedled permission from his brother to borrow a horse and chaise. Then they would go farther in their rambles, enjoying each other's company more and more.

Meanwhile, Henry's school duties had commenced; so he was living in Saugerties at the homes of his various pupils. Alida prolonged her visit with her cousin so that she might see more of the young pedagogue. Those were the days of long visits. An individual or a whole family might descend upon a friend or a relative and spend a week, a month, or six months; and nobody minded. Food was plentiful and cheap; so was household help. Thus, Alida stayed on in Saugerties, and Henry spent every waking hour that he could spare from his duties in her company.

To make a long story short, Henry and Alida were married at the end of six months and settled down in Saugerties. Henry had the steady job of schoolmaster, besides an extra income from his music pupils; also, he continually composed verses and set them to music. It looked as if a rosy future lay ahead of the young couple.

However, the happy glow that surrounded them was to be tragically short. Alida, never very robust, sickened in the second year of their marriage. Her glowing beauty faded, as beauty always does under the onslaught of disease. She became a helpless, querulous invalid. Henry, always faithful and tender, cared for her and took care of the house besides. All that work he did in addition to his school duties and his music lessons. At first, the neighbors tried to help him but they soon found that Alida did not care for their aid. So, one by one, they stopped coming in.

Alida's easy chair was always pushed up to the window, and, before he went to work each morning, Henry would help his wife gently to the window and establish her in her coign of vantage, where, although she could not take any part in the busy life of the community, she could be a spectator, at least.

So the years passed. No longer could Henry roam the woods and fields with Alida and the dogs. He had to hurry home from school to prepare meals, take care of the invalid, and keep the house in some semblance of cleanliness and order. And in spite of all his striving and conniving, there were always bills: doctor bills, food bills, bills for medicine, and little luxuries for his wife, things to keep her contented and happy in spite of the pain and loneliness.

Neighbors, and others of the community, going by to market would see the small white face at the window, day in and day out, year in and year out. They became so accustomed to seeing the thin, shawl-wrapped figure in the same place that it was a shock to everybody when one morning in May, 1845, the chair at the window was empty.

Alida had died peacefully in her sleep. There were many who said it was a mercy, that Alida had lived too long, that her passing had freed Henry from a dreary bondage. Yet, those who knew the Bard best realized that his life would be barren indeed without his beloved wife, even though she had been wife in name only for nearly twenty-five years.

Those who saw Henry Backus at Alida's funeral, and afterward, realized that he was completely bereft. Many who tried to comfort him found him filled with a dreary hopelessness that no words of comfort could assuage.

The Monday morning after the funeral, when the children assembled at the school, they waited in vain for Mr. Backus. The schoolmaster had disappeared. The school board and the neighbors made an investigation. The Backus house was closed and locked. Through the windows the investigators could see the furniture neatly arranged—everything washed, dusted, cleaned, and in its place—but the master of the house had vanished.

For many months, Henry Backus was not seen or heard of; then somebody reported having seen him with his fiddle and two dogs for companions, wandering along one of the less frequented roads of Greene County. After that, at various times, people would tell of having seen him at one place or another, always with his fiddle on his shoulder and his canine friends at his heels; but he never came back to his home.

One night, a breathless, frightened girl rushed into her home in Saugerties shortly after ten in the evening. She had been sent by her mother to borrow some liniment from a neighbor. She had taken a short-cut home past the old Backus house. She declared hysterically that she had seen a face at the window—at the very window where Alida Backus had sat for so many weary years. The face, the girl insisted, was the white, worn face of the schoolmaster's wife.

The next day the house was searched, but it was empty except for the dusty furniture, empty as it had been ever since the Bard had turned the key in the lock and walked out of his old life forever.

After that incident, the place was shunned at night. A few who unthinkingly or brazenly went by after nightfall, reported that they had seen a strange, white face pressed against the window panes. Had Alida Backus come back to sit again at the window where she had sat so long? Perhaps so. Stranger things than that have happened.

Then came the spring of 1861. Henry Backus was found lying in an old shed in Katsbaan—emaciated, sick, dying. He was brought to Saugerties where a charge of vagrancy was preferred against him. He was taken to the Kingston jail, where, after a few days of illness, he died. His body was brought to Saugerties and interred at the town's expense. The remains were placed in the cheapest kind of pine box and hastily dumped into the earth—into the six-foot cavity which is the common portion of all the sons of Adam. His last song had been sung—his story had been told—his earthly journey ended—he was soon to be forgotten.

Or was he? A few weeks after his death, a roistering, jolly crowd, coming home from a party, passed the old Backus house unthinkingly. Suddenly, some member of the group remembered the old legend and looked fearfully toward the front window of the house. It was blank and dark. A small, white face peered into the night. Excitedly, the group told their tale in the village. Then the scoffers rose in legion: There had never been a face, it was the tale of an imaginative, hysterical child, confirmed only by more imaginative, hysterical children.

But a few, thoughtful people believed and said that there *had* been a face—the face of Alida Backus. That for a quarter of a century she had waited at the dark window for her loving, faithful husband, and when he had finally come, her vigil was ended—she needed to wait no more.

Madam Brett's Garden

THE BARE little garden, wrested from the ever encroaching, hungry forest, lay frosted with moonlight that long-ago evening in June, 1709. Roger Brett, Catherina, and their infant child were wrapped in slumber within the snug home which Roger had built with the help of his two slaves. Across the river, the rolling hills, which would finally merge into the Catskills, stretched away to the north. The few log houses, which comprised the Rombout precinct (now the village of Fishkill and the city of Beacon) were dark and silent. The broad bosom of the Hudson, a ribbon of gleaming silver, was quiet and undisturbed.

Darkly on the metallic, motionless strip which was the river, there suddenly appeared a long slender boat, a big boat, moving noiselessly. In it were five men who bent to their oars with such care and precision that it amounted to furtiveness. They moored the craft quietly in a small cove just below the settlement. With scarcely a sound they lifted a small chest from the boat, and four of them bore it between them up the steep bank. The men carried their burden with obvious difficulty. Twice they stopped to rest before the crest of the riverbank was reached. They were panting heavily when they finally set it down in the small clearing a few yards from the river's edge.

"Where's the fort, Mynheer?" whispered one of the burden bearers, a sinister looking man with a bandage around his head which completely covered one eye.

The man addressed was short and stocky. His hair was cut square in the fashion of the Dutch. A broad white collar and belted coat furthermore proved his Holland Dutch origin. His whispered words were in Dutch, which the others seemed to understand, for they shouldered their burden and set off in the direction toward which their leader pointed.

After they had trudged steadily along for several minutes, a small house came into view, a house which apparently stood alone in the wilderness.

"Not so loud," whispered the leader, as one of the men stumbled over a projecting rock, and nearly precipated himself and his burden upon the rocky path.

"S-death, this doesn't look like the place the Captain meant," muttered the man with the bandaged eye. "Not if I know anything, it doesn't. He said an old fortress. This is the Rombout patent, ain't it, Mynheer? That there is Roger Brett's cabin, I'll bet. Hell's bells, after we've waited twelve years to get this loot planted, then we get to the wrong place at the last."

The man addressed as "Mynheer" answered something in Dutch which seemed to placate "One Eye" because he shouldered his burden with the others and plodded on until the five were standing almost under the windows of the Brett house.

With smothered grunts of relief, the men set down their burden and stretched their weary muscles. Meanwhile, the leader had moved somewhat apart from the others and by the bright, clear light of the moon was intently studying a piece of paper which he had drawn from a pocket concealed under his broad, leather belt. With the paper smoothed flat against one of the rough-hewn posts of the garden fence, he was tracing with a stubby forefinger some lines drawn thereon.

The men waited quietly, almost sullenly, for their leader's next move. It came suddenly in an imperious beckoning signal. With the forefinger of his left hand against his bearded lips, the leader guided them down to the farthest end of the spacious garden. There he stopped them beneath the wide-spreading branches of a monstrous oak tree, which must have been centuries old when Christopher Columbus was staring out to sea, a wide-eyed boy, listening to sailors' yarns and dreaming of the far-off day when he, master of his own ship, should set forth to explore the "Sea of Darkness."

Following the leader's whispered directions, the men disappeared in the gloom of the forest from whence they had come. When they had gone, the bearded Dutchman sat down on the little chest and buried his face in his hands. For a long time he sat thus, motionless, under the branches of the great tree. Of a sudden, the snapping of a twig warned him of the return of his men. They were carrying pickaxes and spades. He rose wearily, and with gestures indicated where they should dig.

For an hour they worked while the stocky Dutchman watched, leaning against the trunk of the huge oak. Finally, when the hole reached the size and proportions of a grave, one of the men, with the silent speed of an angry cat, suddenly threw his shovel to the ground, drew a knife from his belt, and lunged for "One Eye." But the motionless watcher was quicker. His own knife flashed in the silver moonlight and buried itself to the hilt in the back of the would-be assassin. With a grunt the man slumped forward on his face.

"One-Eye" and the others had stepped back out of the range of the brief struggle. Now the former stepped forward, aiming a vicious kick at the body of the slain man. The kick thrust the body forward and toppled it with a dull thud into the aperture just made. All four men laughed grimly and silently. Then, with the help of the leader, the three men lowered the chest, where it dropped the last few feet squarely upon the body of the man who had so treacherously sought to kill his companion.

Quickly and quietly the men filled in the grave. After their task was complete, they trampled the earth hard and firm, and scattered grass and gravel until all evidence of their work had become obliterated. Then they picked up their tools and followed the stout Dutchman back through the forest and down the steep bank to the boat. There they embarked, each man taking his oar, the taciturn leader taking the place of the dead man.

Roger Brett and his lady never noticed the trampled spot under the great oak. Often, in later years, Madam Brett, long a widow, would sit there of a Sunday afternoon, marveling at the wondrously beautiful tints of the sunsets which could be glimpsed through the trees. Whoever the slain man had been, he must have slept in peace for he never bothered any member of the Brett household. Madam Brett, herself, was always honored and loved by all, and perhaps her benevolent influence kept at bay the sinister soul who slept unknown and unsuspected at her feet.

Over 250 years have passed since the death of Captain Kidd. Through the passage of time, many places have been variously and erroneously designated as the hiding places of his treasure. Maybe Madam Brett's garden is one of those repositories. It could very well be.

What Became of the Sentry?

IN THE ten-year period, between 1655 and 1665, the people of Wiltwyck (Kingston) and the Esopus Indian tribe had trouble. There was much bloodshed on both sides. Lonely outposts and farms were burned by the redskins, and their families ruthlessly slaughtered. One such outpost was what is called "the old Lowther place" in Mount Marion. I do not think it was that house, but one probably built on the same foundation. When fighting waxed furious, the place was heavily garrisoned, for if it were not well defended everybody knew that all its inmates might be murdered.

Every night a sentry was posted, and for a while all was well. Then one morning a sentry was missing. Not even his body could be found. The garrison was terrified. What could have happened? But the next night a man courageously volunteered for sentry duty. He was accepted and went to his post. The next morning no trace of him could be discovered. The people in the fort were almost crazed with fear. What was happening? Where were their men disappearing? What should be their next move?

At this junction a man came forward and calmly offered himself for sentry duty, on one condition: He should be authorized to shoot anything on sight, anything at all—cat, dog, chicken, man, or woman. The permission was granted him, and that night the sentry took his gun and left the fort. The people inside waited in fear and trembling. Suddenly, through the silence of the night, a shot sounded! Was the sentry killed or had he slain someone? A few of the most daring ones started out to investigate. Halfway between the fort and the stockade they saw a dark figure striding along, dragging something over the ground. The men stiffened and cocked their muskets.

But they had nothing to fear. It was their own sentry. The strange looking thing he was dragging along the ground beside him was apparently a wild boar, many of which in those long-gone days roamed these parts freely. Ferocious and ugly, they would attack even a man if hungry enough. Pushing into the fort for torches the men directed the light upon the animal. To their amazement they saw a swarthy hand where the beast's hoof should have been. Stripping off the skin they disclosed the body of an Indian brave. The redskin had been creeping up on the sentries when at last the third sentry's bullet put an end to his plan, and so defeated the wily cunning of the red man, who had already taken the lives of two of the fort's defenders.

Fulton's Folly and Mrs. Brink's Bonnet

HISTORY GIVES us a clear and truthful picture of the boy Fulton, but none of the history texts in the hands of children today makes mention of the man who made Fulton's Folly something other than folly by his deft and skillful handling. The man who steered that wonder boat on its maiden voyage up the lovely, historic Hudson to Albany and back again was Captain Andrew Brink of Saugerties, one of the most brilliant navigators of his times. He knew the Hudson and he knew engines. And Robert Fulton trusted him implicitly.

Here is the story of the first voyage, and incidentally the story of "Mrs. Brink's Bonnet." It was this way: Fulton started out from New York City on the seventeenth of August, 1807. It was late in the afternoon on Monday. They beat their way all night against tide and wind up the Hudson toward Albany. Late on Tuesday afternoon they arrived at Saugerties. They dropped anchor on the Tivoli side and Fulton went ashore to spend the night with his friend, Chancellor Robert Livingston, at his country estate, Clermont.

Captain Brink had a small boat put over the side, and rowed himself across the river to Saugerties. Here he stayed the night in the home of his father-in-law, where Seamon Park is today. From all accounts, we are led to believe that Captain Brink was an expert engineer, a clever navigator, and a firm and strict officer. But underneath his rather forbidding exterior it is very probable that he was merely a plain, old-fashioned, henpecked husband. And so, when his wife said, "I'm going to Albany with you in the morning," very likely Captain Brink said, "Yes, ma'am."

Accordingly, the next day he took Mrs. Brink down to the shore, placed her in the small boat, and rowed her over to the "Experiment," as Fulton's boat was then called.

The night that had just passed, the night of August 18, 1807, was to be a memorable one in the history of navigation, for during the hours of his stay in Tivoli, Robert Fulton and his rich and powerful friend, Chancellor Livingston, must have had a long and serious talk, because after that maiden voyage of his boat, the inventor had plenty of money to make changes and improvements on the "Experiment." Robert Fulton had brains and inventive genius but very little of this world's goods; so when he changed the name of his famous, little boat from "Experiment" to "Clermont" people realized that he was naming it for Livingston's estate in Tivoli. It is easy to put two and two together and make four as the people of that day soon did. Robert Livingston's wealth had made it possible for Robert Fulton's genius to blossom and bear fruit. The mighty and powerful engines of our day are the great, great-grandchildren of Fulton's tea kettle.

But to return to the "Experiment": She reached Albany at four o'clock Wednesday afternoon. They docked at Saugerties at six o'clock Thursday night and left for New York at seven o'clock Friday morning, arriving at four in the afternoon at their pier in New York City. Thus, another great era in world history was started. But this is not telling yet the story of the Captain's wife and her beautiful bonnet.

As tradition records it, Mrs. Brink was a very attractive woman, and she was truly the apple of her husband's eye. He liked to see her loveliness enhanced by all the finery of the day, and the grace of her small figure emphasized by the most modish of the current fashions. On the day of the memorable trip to Albany she was appropriately garbed in her best, and her costume was surmounted by a huge, satin bonnet, the last word in feminine headgear over a century and a half ago.

Just as the "Experiment" was nosing her way carefully into the Albany port, and thousands and thousands of people, who had come down to the dock to see the great, strange craft, were cheering wildly, something happened.

Mrs. Brink, who was one of the very few women aboard the "Experiment," was standing on deck toward the bow end of the boat. As the day was warm she had untied her bonnet strings. Suddenly a gust of wind lifted the great bonnet and sent it flying over the rail. The Captain's wife gasped and screamed. All for naught! Her lovely blue bonnet, with its salmon-colored, satin ribbons and its gay bird of paradise, went sailing over the port waters, over the heads of the crowd of onlookers, and landed on the second-story window sill of a nearby warehouse. The window was filled with people who eagerly snatched at the brilliant object, but their efforts were fruitless. The bonnet eluded them and plummeted down into the dirty waters of the harbor.

Captain Brink, who was extremely busy down in the engine room, knew nothing of his wife's mishap until he came up on deck to receive, with Robert Fulton, the plaudits of the cheering spectators.

"Andrew," said his wife calmly, "I shall go down below and you will go out and purchase for me a suitable bonnet. Remember, I want one with a bird of paradise."

At these words a look of sympathetic understanding passed between Robert Fulton and his engineer.

When the "Experiment" tied up in the Albany port and her crew and passengers went ashore, Captain Brink was one of their number, but his wife did not accompany him, for it was unthinkable for a lady to be seen bareheaded in public in those days. A few hours later the Captain returned to the boat, and the crew was not surprised to see him bearing in his arms a monstrous big hatbox.

And when, the next day on its way back to New York, the

"Experiment" stopped at Saugerties, Mrs. Brink stepped ashore with a bird of paradise sitting jauntily among the satin folds of her brand-new blue bonnet!

Uncle Hans

WHEN I am inclined to worry about the future or to wonder if I am ever going to accomplish what I have set out to do I think of Uncle Hans and take heart. That sturdy old ancestor of mine lived in the Catskill Mountains, somewhere near the top of the Kaaterskill Clove. And it was a long time ago. There was no graded mountain road, no heavy, rustic fence. There was just a steep, precipitous path. About the beginning of the nineteenth century, traversing the mountain was a real feat; a human being ascending or descending the mountain was like a fly crawling up or down a vertical wall. But the dangerous path held no fears for Uncle Hans. At any hour of day or night he would drop in casually upon members of his family who lived in the valley.

One particularly icy night, when the old man had "unhitched," when the horse was munching his oats in the stable, and Uncle Hans was sitting down to a hearty supper of "relitches" and "Johnny cake," one of the nephews queried: "Uncle Hans, I should think you would be afraid to come down the mountain on a night like this."

Uncle Hans helped himself liberally to apple butter. "No, Peter," he said calmly, "I trust in the Lord and the britchen strap."

Now, in this modern day and age very few people know what a britchen strap is. It is the most important part of a horse's harness. It is the broad, heavy, leather thong which passes behind the horse's hind legs. It must be very strong and it must be fastened very firmly and securely to the rest of the harness, for it supports the entire weight of the animal when he holds back on steep hills. If it should break the load would roll against the beast, causing him to lose his footing or else to run in wild panic. So it must be firm and strong.

And so I make my britchen strap strong. In other words, I do all that I can, and the best that I can, and then I leave the rest to the Lord.

Burgoyne's Ride

IN THE Old Senate House, in Kingston, New York, among the historic relics of our country, is preserved a piece of wood. It is part of a wagon box (probably hickory or white oak, possibly pine). We are not concerned with the wood itself, but of the part it played in American history.

When Burgoyne surrendered to Gates at Saratoga, after the decisive American victory in June, 1777, the English General became very ill. Whether the sickness was the result of his worriment and chagrin over his disastrous defeat, or whether the hardships of wilderness fighting were more than he could take, we have no way of knowing now. But we do know that he was too ill to ride to Albany. He had to be taken and, of course, he was a prisoner of sorts. There was a road into Albany from Saratoga, if it could be dignified by such a name. In actuality it was two, deeply-rutted wagon tracks, between and on either side of which grew tall rank grass, weeds, and bushes. Stones and the stumps of young trees, which had been hastily hacked down to make way for the army, further impeded the wilderness trail. To guide a wagon over such a trail called for skill, a knowledge of the countryside, and a lot of sound, hardheaded Yankee sense.

Two men who possessed these requisites in a high degree were the Myer boys from Saugerties. They were farm boys, brothers, the sons of Christian Myer. (Old Christian, a descendant of the Palatines, those pious, patriotic refugees from the German Rhine, is noted in history for having given twenty-two sons, grandsons, and sons-in-law to fight for the cause of American Independence.)

The Myer brothers accepted calmly the responsibility of taking the defeated British General to Albany. They set out on as lovely a summer day as ever the Hudson Valley had seen, a sturdy farm team pulling the long, boxed wagon, the General lying on an improvised bed, and the brothers on the high seat.

At noontime, on their first day's journey from Saratoga, they stopped in a little clearing to rest the horses and eat. The Myer boys helped the General out of the wagon, spread a blanket on the ground, and eased him down upon it, so that he could be as comfortable as possible. Then they proceeded to unpack a loaf of bread, some cheese, and a side of bacon. After building a fire, they sliced the meat. While one of the boys unhitched and fed the horses, the other roasted the bacon. Soon the appetizing smell of the food tempted even the General, and, propped up against a tree, he did full justice to the woodland meal.

Afterward, while the three men sat smoking sociably, a slight sound startled them. Ever on the alert, the two Myer boys jumped to their feet and seized their muskets. All three looked in the direction from which the sound had come.

Standing beneath a great oak tree nearby was a young Indian — tall, swarthy, straight as an arrow. With a piercing and bold scrutiny, his black eyes rested steadily upon first one and then the other of the men, but his hands were empty. He was not holding bow or rifle. Slowly the boys lowered their guns.

"Look out!" warned Oom Hans, "there may be others."

As if the Indian understood, he walked boldly into the clearing. "No others," he said distinctly.

A look of something like recognition flashed into John Burgoyne's eyes.

"What do you want?" growled Oom Hans.

"Eat," said the Indian simply.

The Myer boys were kindhearted, and, although they were not quite sure, they trusted the Indian and they gave him food.

While eating, he said nothing, but his strange fathomless eyes rested upon first one and then the other of the men. Suddenly with one single graceful motion he rose. Looking at Burgoyne and pointing first to the west, he said solemnly, "No come." Then pointing to the south he repeated the phrase. The long brown finger pointed at Burgoyne. "White men all go," he said, "back across the water." Looking at Oom Hans and his brother he said, "White man spread over all country." His arm made a vague gesture toward the west. "Red men go, too." he said sadly, "Nowhere to go."

With another muttered word, which none of the men understood, the Indian abruptly turned and vanished into the forest fastness. So quick were his movements—and silent —that he seemed almost to melt into thin air.

The Myer brothers laughed. "Queer duck," said Oom Hans. But Burgoyne was strangely silent. The camaraderie, which the meal seemed to have inspired, had fallen from him. His face was set in grim lines of hopelessness. When the boys helped him back into the wagon they fancied he was delirious, for they heard him murmur, "In vain, in vain, all to no avail."

The rest of the trip to Albany was uneventful, except that the General spoke no more, not a single word to either of the boys unless they asked him a direct question; then he answered as briefly as possible.

People thought it strange that Burgoyne showed no surprise at the news of St. Leger's defeat, and the failure of Howe to come up from New York. Many thought that his apathetic acceptance of the tidings was the result of the combination of his own failure to accomplish his mission and his physical illness. Yet the Myer brothers of Saugerties might have explained his indifference had they cared to speak.

Whoever the strange Indian was, he had prophesied truly for the British, for the Americans, and for his own harried race.

The Minister

THE REVEREND MR. JOHNSON stirred uneasily. The words of his Sunday sermon would not come. The plush of the elegant "spring rocker," his wife's wedding dues had purchased, pricked through the white cambric of his shirt. He mopped his brow and stared into space. The golden sunshine of a perfect June day splashed the green lawn of the parsonage. The wheels of a lumber wagon rattled noisily over the planks of the bridge. A bird sang with joyous abandon on the bough of the tulip tree beside his window.

Elder Johnson arose. "Julia," he called, "where is Sally? Shall we go out in the boat? It's a lovely afternoon. A row up the creek will take the cobwebs from my brain."

These were the words that ushered in Saugerties' tragic murder mystery—a mystery truly to this day. A century has passed—the actors in the drama, their children and their children's children are dead and forgotten. But a great poet once said, "The evil that men do lives after them."

Mr. Johnson, his wife, and little daughter had come to Saugerties in January, 1852. This was June, 1853. Already the tongues of the village gossips were wagging. Elder Johnson had been seen with Eliza Bolford, walking and talking in the cool of the evening on a secluded path beside the Esopus Creek, not once but many times. The minister was tall and handsome and young. Eliza was pretty and pert—a young servant in the family of one of the rich mill owners in town. She was ignorant and illiterate. What the Elder saw in her, besides a pretty face and a graceful young body, nobody could imagine. But there were many who said that Johnson was a man before he was a minister, that the lovely Eliza had captivated him with her charms and he had fallen. Poor

Mrs. Johnson, with her pale straight hair, her colorless lips and cheeks, and her lank figure, was no match for the seductive Eliza.

But on that June afternoon the family forgot their problems. The creek was a shining, curving ribbon of glass between its tall green banks. Mr. Johnson, who was a clever oarsman, and who loved the water, often took his family out for long leisurely trips up the creek and even on the river. This particular afternoon nobody saw them go but many saw them return—Elder Johnson with his little daughter clasped in his arms. The minister was wild-eyed, dripping wet, and he clutched his daughter convulsively to his breast. He reported that somehow during their row back from the picnic, his wife had gone overboard. As he told it, she had unexpectedly stood up, the boat had tipped, and she had fallen into the creek. He had made every effort to save her but her heavy skirts had dragged her down. Though he had rowed round and round several times she had not come to the surface. That was his story, and that was the story he steadfastly maintained as the whole truth of the matter.

Later his wife's body was recovered and an impressive funeral was held. Feeling ran high. Many people thought that the minister was concealing the true facts. His congregation treated him coldly and suspiciously, so he and his young daughter left town. Shortly thereafter, Eliza Bolford moved away. Nobody knew exactly where she went or why. But in a year or so rumors began to float. Somebody reported that the minister and Eliza were married. Neither was ever heard from again, so maybe they were married.

But to return to the tragedy! Probably, at first, not a soul in the village would have suspected anything, and, with the burial of the unfortunate lady, the distressing incident would have been closed. But the unwitting question of an innocent, wide-eyed child opened the eyes of the community to the criminal aspect of the episode.

One day, shortly after the death of his wife, while the Reverend Mr. Johnson was relating the details of the "accident" to a member of his flock, his small daughter looked up earnestly into his face and said: "Papa, why did you push Mama with the oar when she tried to get back into the boat?"

"Boots" Van Steenburgh

HE PICKED himself up and carefully dusted off his Sunday suit, which had scraped over the sidewalk and had become very dirty and torn. He looked around for his hat disregarding the jeering laughs of the bystanders. Pa had paid a dollar and a half for that hat. He must not go home without it. Where was his necktie? Oh, yes, here, up under his coat collar toward the back. And last night his shirt had been torn. He had tried to mend it after he had climbed the four steep flights of stairs to his lodgings. Lucky Ma had put in an extra one, for he hadn't made very good progress with the needle. He stood uncertainly on the curb looking longingly toward the theater.

"Come now, get goin', lad," said a rough voice, and a policeman gave him a not unkindly shove. "You're not the only one that loves Jenny Lind, you know. Got lotsa company."

And so "Boots" Van Steenburgh became one of our local celebrities. The older generation can remember him as a very old man when they were children. He was never called anything but "Boots," for winter and summer, year in and year out, he wore high leather boots.

During the latter part of his life he was mentally deranged and practically penniless. He wandered aimlessly about the countryside, often stopping at schoolhouses and asking the teachers if he might address the children. When granted permission he would implore the children, with strange words and gestures, to do good, to love their parents, their country, and their God. But his words were so disjointed and wild that nearly always he provoked laughter rather than respect.

When he was young it was said that he was perfectly normal mentally. He was tall and good looking and fairly well-to-do, judging by the rural standards of the times. "Boots" would probably have lived out his days in comfort with a wife selected from among the neighbor girls if it had not been for the advent of the Swedish Nightingale. That was in 1853, over a century ago. And Castle Garden, the famous old theater at the tip of Manhattan beyond Battery Park, was crowded to capacity as long as that golden voice was lifted.

"Boots" heard of her beauty, of her magnetic personality, and above all, of her wondrous voice. The farm boy, who loved music, vowed that he would go to the big city and hear the golden bird that was imprisoned in the Swedish girl's white throat. Far better for him had he stayed home and followed the plow as it turned the brown furrow in the upland meadow beyond his childhood home.

But he went down to New York. The city must have been bewildering to the simple country boy. In the middle of the nineteenth century New York was not the vast place it is today, but it was no country town. It was one of the biggest cities in the world. Poor "Boots" must have been confused and amazed by the sights and sounds of the teeming metropolis. Yet somehow he found his way to Castle Garden where Jenny Lind sang each night to thousands of people.

He listened to the voice which had cast its spell over millions, and the infatuated lad vowed he would see the singer and talk to her. He made his way past the hangers-on at the back door of the theater. They snickered audibly at the awkwardness of the gawky country boy, painfully shy, dressed up in his Sunday best to come to the Big Town. However, "Boots" cared nothing for them, did not see them, did not hear them. One burning desire filled his heart—to see Jenny Lind face to face, to touch her hand. Then he would be satisfied, and not till then. After that, he would go back home and spend all the rest of his days toiling in the fields. But, ah, his nights would be free to dream of Jenny.

Poor Boots! He never did get past the guards that surrounded the great singer. They would not let him in. In fact, he was thrown out bodily by the stalwart police who were set to keep out just such intruders as he. For several days he lingered around the stage door, but when he finally realized that his utmost efforts were in vain, he gave up in despair and returned to Saugerties.

After his return, folks began to notice that Boots was getting "queer." He talked wildly and incoherently at times. He paid no attention to his personal appearance. For several years he grew gradually worse. After the death of his parents, he seemed to sink deeper into his odd ways. He sold or gave away his home; perhaps he lost it for debt, for he no longer worked. He moved into a little shack on the Glasco road (the lower road to Kingston). I think he must have made this shanty with his own hands, for it was simply thrown together —a rough, board affair with the cracks plastered over with mud.

As the years went swiftly onward, Boots grew more unkempt and ragged (if that were possible). His long white hair and beard floated over his shoulders and chest, and the rags of his nondescript garments waved in the wind as he roamed the woods and fields or plodded along the highways. Often he talked to himself and gestured with his dirty, claw-like hands. But he was harmless. Nobody feared the poor old creature. Everybody was kindly and tolerant toward Boots.

One evening in the early spring when Boots was near the end of his earthly pilgrimage, a boy of twelve or thereabouts, who had been sent by his mother on an errand, went whistling toward Boots's little cabin. When near the shack the lad stopped his whistle and crept softly to the window to peep in upon the old man. The boy meant to give the lonely old hermit a friendly hail and "pass the time of day," for Boots had endeared himself to all the children of the community.

In spite of his good intentions, when he reached the window, the youth could not see inside, for the dust, smoke, and filth of a generation had collected upon the small panes.

"Boots must have company," mused Jack for the sound of

Folklore of the Hudson Valley 55

voices was clearly audible. The rumbling tones of Boots's harsh old voice fell upon the boy's ears, and then, suddenly, in the pause that followed, that of another voice.

Slowly the hair began to rise on Jack's startled young head, his hands clenched, and his eyes bulged in horror. The unearthly sweetness of the second voice held him spellbound. Then softly upon the evening air floated the aria of one of the great operas (had Jack only known it), the aria of a great opera sung in an unknown tongue, sung in a woman's voice so sweet that the evening thrush stopped to listen.

When the voice finally sank into silence, Jack stood transfixed for one moment of breathless horror. Indelibly was stamped upon his soul the conviction that the tones he had just heard were not those of any human voice. With a great leap he cleared the tiny yard in one bound and was off down the road at such incredible speed that he arrived pale and panting at his destination. Nor would he answer the neighbor's kindly questions as to what had scared him. Jack was not a timid boy and the neighbor was puzzled to see him in a state of such abject fear.

Many years afterward, when he was a grown man, Jack confessed to the thing that had frightened him on the balmy evening of that long-gone springtime.

One day, a couple of years after the incident just related, it occurred to several of the neighbors that they had seen nothing of Boots for a long time. Inquiry of persons living nearest him brought out the fact that there had been no sign of life around the shack for a long time. But this, in itself, meant nothing, for Boots would be gone sometimes for weeks (in good weather) tramping about the countryside, stopping at the schools and gatherings where young people were apt to congregate, to harangue the boys and girls about love of flag and country.

But this absence had been so long as to warrant investigation. The latch of the sagging door of the old hovel was lifted and several of the neighbors trooped in. As soon as they had stepped over the threshold, the men of the invading party removed their hats quickly and reverently in deference to the Presence presiding in that humble room.

Boots was lying on his rickety bed, the blanket pulled up to his chin, and his grizzled, bearded head turned sidewise on the pillow. Somewhere beyond the gates of Eternity, he must have found his Jenny, for the expression on his face was one of ineffable joy and peace.

Cornplanter Abeel

THE CHIEF of the Senecas was not happy when he learned that a paleface had been looking upon his daughter, Alequipsis, with desire in his eyes and heart. When he angrily confronted John Abeel, the younger, with the accusation that he had been making love to an Indian princess, the young man coolly confessed that such was the case. Furthermore, he astounded the old Chieftain by the assertion that he meant, with her father's consent, to marry the Indian maiden and carry her off to his own wigwam in the "white" country.

The Indian, a king among his own people, sent for his daughter. She confirmed what young John had said, and stoutly maintained that she loved him and meant to follow him into the white man's country. The Chieftain loved his daughter, and he had but one recourse. Preparations for the marriage were immediately started. For nearly a week there was feverish activity in the camp of the Senecas. Then the marriage feast was begun after the day-long ceremony and tribal dance. For three days and three nights the feasting went on.

Then John Abeel and his bride turned their horses' heads to the eastward and started on the first lap of their long journey into the "white" country. All the Indians, braves and squaws alike, were horrified when John Abeel insisted that his young bride should ride one of the pack horses that he had brought with him when he had come on his trading mission into the Indian country. It was unthinkable that a squaw should ride. She should walk behind and carry the excess baggage. But Abeel firmly insisted that his wife was not a squaw. She was the wife of a white man, the wife of John Abeel, and as such she must be treated.

On their arrival at the home of his father, pandemonium broke loose. John Abeel, Senior, denounced his son for a crazy fool who had fallen under the spell of a pair of brilliant pagan eyes. But John, Junior, was not to be cowed or browbeaten. He stood up to his father as he had stood up to the Indian Chief. And in the end he won. By wily persuasion as well as by dogged determination, he overcame his father's objections. One point though, his father gained. They must be married by the white man's ceremony. No son of his should take to him a wife, be she heathen or Christian, unless they stood before the Dutch dominie, plighted their troth, and repeated their vows. Eventually so it was. The young couple journeyed to Albany and in the little Dutch church beneath the spreading elms the dominie made them man and wife in the sight of God and man. Then, once more, John Abeel and his wife set forth on their journey to his father's home.

Meanwhile, John Senior, who, in spite of his raving, had been favorably impressed with his lovely daughter-in-law, had been thinking things over from a materialistic, as well as a paternal standpoint. An Indian daughter-in-law would not be a bad investment. Much wealth was to be derived from the Indian country, and having his son connected to the red men by marriage ties was not a bad idea at all. Moreover, the girl was beautiful and gentle, all a man could wish for in a woman. Abeel had never looked down upon the Indians as many of the more ignorant white men did. He realized that they were a great people and an intelligent race. He respected them, as they in turn, respected him; and so, when John Junior returned from Albany with his dark-eyed, red-lipped bride, John Senior was standing on the great stone slab which formed the doorstep of the palatial log house which was his home. As their horses plodded wearily up to the door, John

Abeel stepped up to his daughter-in-law's horse, grasped the bridle and stopped it. Then he held up his arms, and the frightened, lonely, little princess, who had become a white man's wife, somehow understood the gesture, for she slid gratefully down into the protection of those strong arms.

John Junior loved his wife with a deep and abiding love, and loved her to the day of his death, as a husband should. John Senior gave her the tender love which he would have lavished upon a daughter if he had had one. Always there was a strong tie of affection between those two which was never broken. When her son was born and she insisted upon giving him the name "Cornplanter," her husband was deeply affronted. He called it "heathen nonsense." But her father-in-law upheld her. He, as well as John Junior, would have liked the boy to be called "John" or "David," old names in the Abeel family, but if his beloved daughter wanted it "Cornplanter," then "Cornplanter" it should be.

Both men were thankful in the years to come that they had yielded to the Indian girl's wishes, for Cornplanter became a great man, both in the Indians' eyes and in the eyes of the white people. Many and many a time he averted impending war by his easy access to the Indian country, by his knowledge of Indian ways and customs, and his understanding of the different tribal dialects. The fact that he was an Indian by blood caused the red men to respect his wishes as they would never have respected the wishes of a white man. They listened to him and took his advice. He went into their villages and lived with them. Perhaps not even Sir William Johnson had so much influence over all the tribes of the Iroquois, and especially the Senecas, whose blood ran in his veins, as did Chief Cornplanter.

And so the name, Cornplanter Abeel, is one that should be familiar to all New Yorkers and Pennsylvanians, for without his help those great states could not have climbed to the places they hold today. Harried by the Iroquois, if the tribe had fought with the French in the Colonial wars, we might have been defeated. Give the credit to Sir William Johnson, but give the credit also, to the man who, being half Indian, somehow managed to stay loyal both to his mother's people and those of his father's race.

The lot of the Indian has ever been a sad one. Of all the minority races on the face of the earth perhaps the Indian is the most tragic. Once he was king of a whole continent. Once his proud legions roamed unafraid throughout thousands of miles of forest and plain. Then came the white man with his horses and his guns, and the reign of the Indian was terminated. He did not yield easily. He fought furiously until fighting proved to no avail. Then he sought some form of compromise which would not take from him every last vestige of human dignity. But it was a vain effort. He was alloted skimpy bits of land, his people were huddled together in filth and squalor on "reservations." In despair the red man sank into apathetic resignation.

The story of young John and his Indian princess makes a very lovely and romantic-sounding narrative. The facts about Chief Cornplanter and the great and lasting benefits which New York State and Pennsylvania derived at his hands are true. However, the romantic angle is far from true. John Abeel put away his Indian wife in later years and married a white woman, Mary Knouts, who was orphaned in Brant's massacre at Fort Plain. That would lead us to believe that Abeel and Alequipsis were married only by the Indian ceremony, which, no matter how binding it seemed in the eyes of the red men, was not legal by the white man's standards. But all that is beside this issue. Anyone descended from Cornplanter Abeel, or connected in any way by blood to that distinguished mediator should be proud indeed. Cornplanter married and was the father of one son, Jesse Cornplanter Abeel.

Cornplanter died in 1836, being well over a century old. Long before his death the Commonwealth of Pennsylvania had granted him a tract of land in acknowledgment of his successful efforts in keeping the peace between the red men and their white brothers. He spent his declining years in

Warren County, Pennsylvania. His grave there is honored by a special marker, given by the people of the Quaker State, to do homage to a man they wished to pay a lasting tribute of respect and gratitude.

The Tale of the Murdered Slave Girl

CAPTAIN SALISBURY of Leeds, New York, was considered by the neighboring farmers as belonging to the gentry. He was a large landholder, had many servants and was thought to be very wealthy. He had fought under Schuyler in the Revolution, and had a good military record. Nevertheless, he was not popular with his neighbors. People did not like him. He was too overbearing and haughty to be liked by the farmers 'round the countryside.

Salisbury had many servants, and as far as anyone knew or could observe, he treated them well; but one day it was broadcast over the countryside that a young girl belonging to Salisbury had run away. Whether she had been punished for something and frightened, or whether she had been ill treated, nobody know. Some surmised that she might have run off to join her lover, a servant on an adjacent farm. But all this was guesswork. Her escape was published in the paper in the county seat, Catskill, and a reward was offered for any information that might lead to her capture.

After a little over a week had elapsed, a young lad drew rein at Salisbury House. He had come with information concerning the escaped slave girl. A farmer in Tannersville, at the top of the mountain, had seen a dim figure lurking near one of his outbuildings just at dusk. Riding hard, he had overtaken the fleeing girl. She was nearly famished, so weak from lack of food that she could scarcely stand, much less run. He fed her and tied her securely to a post in the barn. Then he sent his son on their best horse, posthaste, to notify Captain Salisbury. The Captain gave the man food and drink and kept him overnight. The next morning he set out with the Tannersville man for the mountain, after first winding a long coil of stout rope about his saddlehorn.

When they reached the home of the Tannersville farmer, Salisbury opened his wallet and paid the mountain man the reward he had offered, also he paid him for his trip down the mountain, and the food given the girl. This, of course, was done after the Captain had seen for himself that the woman held was really his servant. Then, after a few hours rest and food for himself and his horse, Captain Salisbury fastened the girl, by a length of the rope he had brought with him, securely to the horn of his saddle. His intentions were to make the girl walk home to Salisbury House as part of her punishment for running away. I say those were his intentions. The slave girl was weak from her exhausting flight and lack of food, and try as she would, she could not walk as fast as the Captain's high-blooded horse. Every few steps Salisbury was forced to rein in his horse and wait for the girl to get breath and strength to go on. After a little bit of this, master and steed became very restive. Remember, all this happened over 150 years ago. It could be this is not exactly as it really occurred, as these old folk tales become garbled in the passage of the years. I can only tell it as it was told to me. The Captain's horse bolted. Probably something at the roadside frightened him, or perhaps the slave girl fainted and fell against him. Anyhow he ran away and dragged her to her death. When Salisbury finally succeeded in stopping him, the girl was a mass of battered flesh. There was no life in her body.

When the news was loosed over the countryside, indignation ran high. Salisbury was not popular among the people of these parts. Then, too, justice and mercy, and a feeling for the oppressed have always burned strong in the hearts of the Low Dutchers. The whole Hudson Valley was roused. The Captain was put in the county jail to await his trial. His family secured counsel for him—the best legal mind in the state. When his case came to trial, his lawyer pleaded with all the eloquence at his command. He pointed out that Salisbury had not meant to kill the girl, had not even intended to hurt her in any way. All in vain! The Captain was sentenced to hang. The case was appealed, and once more Salisbury was given the death sentence. But, at the last, a clause was added which saved the Captain from the hangman's noose. No, it didn't either. For all the rest of his life he was to wear a rope about his neck, waking and sleeping. And on his one hundreth birthday he was to be hanged. So the judge pronounced the sentence, and so it was carried out.

The most fantastic part of the whole story is that he lived to be ninety-nine years old. During all those long years, wearing the rope which many thought he deserved, I wonder if he didn't often wish that his life had been snuffed out like that of the hapless slave girl.

A Pin in Her What?

MY GRANDMOTHER was a very remarkable woman I've often heard my father say. Of course, all men remember their mothers as some sort of super beings. Wonderful cooks. Wonderful housekeepers. And the wives down through the generations have groaned and held their heads, or thrown the thing nearest to their hands, according to their temperament.

But many people besides my father have sung Caroline Hommell's praises, so I have come to believe that truly she must have been a woman far beyond her times. She read and she listened in a day when women were supposed to do neither. She bore thirteen children and raised twelve of them. When her long, busy work day was over, when most women would have been satisfied to sit down by the hearthside and knit she was not content. She must know what was going on in the community and in the country. Her advice was sought by many, men and women alike. She could express herself lucidly and beautifully, and words alone did not suffice her. Her deeds were many, generous, and kind.

Wherever there was sorrow or suffering, there she could be found ministering to those in need.

So, one day when the doctor's gig went up the road Grandmother was troubled. Somebody must be sick up at the Freligh's, as theirs was the only house in that direction. Who could it be? Perhaps she could help in some way. She waited impatiently for the doctor's return. Every once in a while she would go to the door to look anxiously up the road. Finally, the doctor's gray horse came in sight over the hill, jogging along in that deceptively, leisurely-looking trot, which could so suddenly change to a flashing dash of speed and carry the old doctor and his dusty, shabby gig over the ground with astonishing rapidity.

Grandmother seized her sunbonnet, opened the door, and hurried across the lawn. "Doctor Brink, oh, Doctor Brink!" she called. "Is there somebody sick up at Freligh's?"

Doctor Brink sawed methodically on the gray mare's reins. He did not bother to turn his head. "Libbie!" he shouted laconically, without halting the gig.

Grandmother, who was built on the short, stout plan, ran a few steps farther. "Well, what's the matter with her?" she asked at the top of her lungs.

"Pin in her ear," called Doctor Brink, morosely.

Grandmother was beginning to grow alarmed. The doctor's gig was getting dangerously close to the brow of the hill. In about a half minute he would disappear and she had not caught his last word. "A pin in her *what*?" she screamed.

"A pin in her *ear!*" thundered the short-tempered, old physician.

Just as the mare quickened her pace Grandmother also panted forward in a last desperate spurt of speed. "Did you get it out?" she yelled.

The gig was vanishing over the first of the many hills which descended in a series of abrupt steps below Mount Airy to the valley beneath.

"Would I leave it in?" queried the doctor, grimly.

So Grandmother Hommell's curiosity was appeased and her mind set at rest, but to the end of her long and useful life her fun-loving family never ceased to tease her about *"a pin in her what?"*

The Forgotten Gravestone

WHEN THE old Maxwell House was pulled down in 1945, there was more than one mystery uncovered. Standing close against the east wall, not more than two feet from the foundation of the building, completely hidden by brush and shrubbery, was a tall bluestone slab. It was a gravestone, for the epitaph was very clearly discernible. Now, why would a gravestone stand against the rear wall of the Maxwell House? Had there been a body buried in the yard?

> Sacred to the memory of Lottie Pell
> Beloved wife of Joseph B. Turner
> Died January 10, 1870
> Aged 30 years, 2 months and 10 days

Up in the hills below Mount Airy there is a small community called Hommellville. In the days just preceding the Civil War, there was a family named Pell living in a snug, little stone house on the first of the plateaus below the old Hommell homestead. That family consisted of the father, mother, and five very beautiful daughters. The "Pell Girls" were renowned the countryside about for their good looks, their wit, and their general high spirits. In fact, it was remembered by folks who lived in that day that the boys from the nearby settlement of Quarryville beat a well-worn path through the woods, ending at the Pell doorstep. All four of the older girls married well; but Lottie, the youngest and comeliest of the five, "Came through the woods and picked up a crooked stick," as my grandmother would say.

Not that there was anything wrong or bad about Joe

Turner. In fact, he was well meaning and kind, but just unfortunate. Poor Joe never started any kind of venture that didn't end in miserable failure. He worked hard but somehow things never seemed to "come his way." His young wife tried hard to make ends meet, but misfortune constantly dogged their footsteps. With the coming of their two boys, life became even more difficult, there being two more mouths to feed.

Joe had a job at the Phoenix Hotel, in 1869, as handyman, doing almost anything about the place. At that time, Lottie conceived the idea of "helping out"; and, although Joe protested, she gave her two little boys into the care of her sister and took up her post as one of the kitchen girls at the hotel. Her family was very bitter about the fact that she had to "work out" and blamed poor Joe for all the hard luck which had pursued Lottie since her marriage.

The months passed, and Lottie and Joe continued to work at the hotel. Their combined earnings enabled them to support themselves and the two children comfortably.

One winter night, when Lottie was scrubbing the big kitchen floor, she was taken suddenly and violently ill. A doctor was sent for immediately; and, although he fought valiantly all night for her life, when morning dawned, the young mother and her baby girl lay dead in one of the back bedrooms of the Maxwell House, or the Phoenix Hotel, as it was called in those days.

Joe's heart was broken. He could not be coaxed to eat or sleep. For long hours he sat in the cold room beside his wife's body, his eyes riveted to her dead face, which had lost all its lines of pain and care, and, in its lovely peace looked again like the face of the gay-hearted girl he had courted.

At last his friends came in, removed him by force as gently as they could and bore Charlotte (Lottie) Turner's body and that of her infant daughter, to the snowbound cemetery.

As soon as Lottie was laid in the grave, Joe went to the nearby marble yard, selected a bluestone slab, and dictated the epitaph; but weeks went by, and months went by, and Joe had made no further move. The marble dealer sought him several times, told him the price of the stone, and asked a small down payment; but Joe didn't have it. Each time he promised vaguely that he would try to make a payment soon. He continued to do odd jobs about the hotel and managed to pay for the support of his two boys, who were living with his sister-in-law. Her antagonistic attitude toward him made it difficult and sometimes impossible for him to see very much of his two young sons. Kate held a cold grudge in her heart against Joe. Upon him she put all the blame for her sister's untimely death.

After a year or so news got about that Joe was "paying attention" to a comely widow. The marble dealer gave up his importunities in disgust. He felt that Joe had forgotten his wife and didn't want to be reminded of her. That may be true or untrue. Whichever it was, don't judge poor Joe too harshly. Remember, he was lonely, and he had two sons whose companionship he had craved for many months and been denied. He was earning more and was well able to marry and take the boys into his own home.

Suddenly the marble dealer had an inspiration. He would appeal to Lottie's sister. He did so with immediate results, but not those he had anticipated. Kate looked with contempt on the bluestone slab. "Beloved wife!" she said bitterly. She purchased a small marble shaft and had it placed at the head of Lottie's grave. So the dealer, thinking the incident closed, leaned the bluestone slab against the fence and forgot it.

Years passed by. Joe settled down to hard, steady work, prospered, and in due time, married the widow. His boys grew to manhood and moved away from Saugerties. Finally Joe died, and the years rolled on. His widow, his boys, and their families passed also. Then came the year 1945. Seventy-five years had gone. Lottie Turner had been dust in the cemetery for three quarters of a century.

Now comes the strangest part of this tragic story. The Maxwell House was sold and razed. When it was pulled down, close to its east wall was found a bluestone slab: "Sacred to the memory of Lottie Pell, Beloved wife of Joseph B. Turner. . . ." Where had the stone been seventy odd years and more? What unknown hand had placed it where it was found? Was there a significance in its being put in that very spot? Nobody will ever answer these questions, for death has sealed the lips of all who could.

Civil War Tales

ONE BLUSTERY day in January, 1865, my grandmother came down to breakfast greatly perturbed, and, to her solicitous family seemed almost frantically worried. On being questioned by her daughters she confessed that she had had a dream. In that dream she had seen David (my father), her son in the Union Army, walking barefoot over snow. Now, my father at that time was with the Army of the Potomac, besieging Petersburg, in Virginia. In vain her daughters reminded Grandmother that there was no snow in Virginia. She would not be convinced by that statement or turned aside from her set purpose. After the breakfast was cleared away Grandmother got out her knitting needles and those of her daughters. Then the wool was produced and all started knitting. The girls thought it was rather silly, but decided it was best to humor their mother. In short order several pairs of heavy woolen socks were completed and sent to David, carefully and correctly addressed: Private David W. Hommell, Company G, 120th Regiment, New York Volunteers' Army of the Potomac, Virginia.

A shivering, six-foot lad thankfully put on the socks a week later. Virginia had had an unprecedented snowfall. The soles of David's shoes were worn through. His socks were gone also. His feet were literally in the snow. Grandmother's premonition had saved her son untold suffering. Perhaps it had saved his life. Nobody but the Maker of mothers will ever know.

"Dave, I'm going to get mine tomorrow." The speaker was a small, thin lad with a sensitive face and expressive dark eyes. The man, or rather boy, to whom he was talking, was broad and tall with merry, blue eyes and a good-humored quirk on his generous mouth.

"Now, now, Saul, that bullet may be marked with my name just as well as yours. Don't get downhearted. There's a hell of an awful battle coming and, if I don't miss my guess, it's going to keep right on for a goodish spell, either until we've licked the Johnnies or they've licked us. However, that doesn't mean that either or both of us must be killed. Somebody is coming out alive, and it can just as well be you and me as anybody else." Dave lifted his great hand and gave his buddy a resounding whack on the back which almost toppled the smaller man off his feet.

The two boys were making supper (hardtack, worm-infested bacon, and dried beans). They were crouched over a campfire, one of thousands which dotted the hills around the insignificant little village of Gettysburg (which in two short days would take its proud place in history with Waterloo, with Valley Forge, with Thermopylae, with all the great shrines of the world where men have died to protect their homes and loved ones, or to maintain the truth of those principles which they deemed to be right).

Saul paid no attention to his friend's reply. It was as if he had not heard him. "Now, listen, Dave," he said earnestly. "I've a few things which I want you to take back to Belle, and to my mother. I won't give them to you tonight if you think I'm being morbid about this. They are in my left-hand pocket. I'll be beside you in every charge we make. Don't stop even if you should see me fall, but go back after the battle, whenever it's safe, and get the little remembrances that I want to send home. Yes, Dave, and tell Belle, if you can, how much I love her. We would have been so happy together. Take the little treasures back to her and Mother. I know you'll do that for me, pard."

For one instant a blur of tears obscured the bright blueness of David's eyes. He seized one of Saul's slight hands in both of his big ones. "I'll do it, Sauley," he whispered, "but heaven grant it won't be necessary."

No more was said on the topic. The boys ate their supper, wrapped themselves in their blankets, and lay down beside their dying campfire. Mosquitoes and moths fluttered about them. In the wheatfields and the peach orchard nearby the locusts set up their droning plaint. Owls hooted mournfully; but the two great armies slept on. Before another nightfall thousands of these boys would be sleeping another kind of sleep, so deep and so peaceful that all the bugles of all the world would never rouse them. Such are the wages of war!

The next morning all was bustle and activity in the two great camps. There was a momentary lull during the breakfast period. Then the great guns were trained each on the other. Men were drawn up in battle formation on each side and the conflict was resumed. Cavalry and infantry of both armies did their part. There were charges and counter charges. The wild "Rebel yell" resounded again and again. Dave and Saul were in the thick of the battle. Attack after attack was made by their brigade and each time the boys were unscathed. Dave's cap was shot away and a bullet tore through his knapsack. Saul wasn't touched. Dave began to be thankful that his buddie's hunch had been wrong. He looked about him. All around him men were piled up, wounded, dead, dying. The agonized screams of men and horses, mingled with the awful sobbing roar of the guns made David's blood run cold. But he was not afraid. He was too excited to be afraid. Once more they were forming to charge. Where was Saul? Where was Saul? David breathed a sigh of relief. There was Saul, safe at his side. Safe? A shell burst, scattering its fragments about them. A seemingly small piece struck the slight figure. Saul stumbled, seemed to be regaining his balance, stumbled again, and this time he went down. All this David saw without turning his head, with his bayonet fixed, madly charging with the rest of his brigade. There was no time to stop, no time to help or lift the body of his stricken comrade. David set his mouth in a hard, straight line and his blue eyes were bleak.

After the brigade had fallen back and the stretcher bearers were going out, David clenched his hands tightly and ran up that terrible slope again. There was Saul, lying peacefully on his side as if he were sleeping. His face was not disfigured, and only the dark stain on the front of his jacket told of his mortal injury. David knelt down beside the body of the man who had been dearer than a brother to him. He didn't know that tears were streaming down his face when he raised his head to give it a negative shake to the stretcher bearers who had paused uncertainly beside Saul's body. David's hand fumbled clumsily inside the tunic which was wet with a sickening, warm stickiness. His fingers closed over a small packet. He drew it out. It was wrapped carefully and unharmed. Mechanically, David laid the package down on the soggy ground beside him. Then he leaned over Saul and carefully buttoned the coat of his uniform. The cap was gone, but with gentle fingers he smoothed the dark, ruffled hair.

"Get back, Yank, we're firing again." A gray-clad figure ran past him and headed up the hill.

David picked up the package and rose. He did not look again at the crumpled, blue-clad figure at his feet. What was the good? Saul was gone. That was the flesh that had housed him for a few short years. It was not his pard. Tomorrow, perhaps he would join his friend. Or it might be fifty, sixty, or seventy years. Sometime, somewhere, they would be together again. Of that David was certain. He ducked and ran down the long incline so hideously cluttered.

David delivered the package on his next furlough. He survived the years of war, came home, settled down, established himself in business, married, and was as good a husband and father as he had been a soldier.

But Belle, Saul's sweetheart—what of her? She was young and lovely. Others sought her, and, in time, she married a wealthy man, one who could provide for her abundantly and well. It might have been that she sought to dull in worldly ease and riches the pain in her heart. The old proverb says: "Time heals all." It is possible that she was the kind who could forget, but I like to think that a part of her lies forever beside Saul in his narrow grave on the sloping hills of Gettysburg.

The Story of Night John

HE WAS really called Night John or Nachte Jan, as the Low Dutchers would say, because he was never seen except at night. His home was a cave in the limestone ledges around Kaatsbaan. (This is beside the topic. That region was called by the Hollanders, the "kaat's baan," which means in English, "the cat's path," for numerous wild cats had their homes there and prowled over the rocks by night and day.) But to get back to Nachte Jan: In Revolutionary days there was a man named Cornelis Persen who kept a store in Kaatsbaan. His home still stands today, mute testimony to the careful workmanship and good materials used by the Low Dutch. Truly they built their houses "upon the rocks."

This Cornelis Persen must have been a good man, humane and kind, for one of his firmest friends was old Nachte Jan, the Indian. Probably Persen had fed the old redskin at various times, very likely seeing to it that the Indian was never in want. Now, there is an old saying that an Indian never forgets a kindness and he never forgives a wrong. Cornelis Persen, in his careless kindness to the old Indian, never thought, expected, or wanted to be repaid. But this is the way life has been since the beginning of time. You "cast your bread upon the waters and after many days it will return to you."

There came a time when Persen sorely needed help. He was an ardent patriot, and the Tories and their Indian allies had sworn to "get him." They had their plans carefully made and all would have gone as expected if they hadn't forgotten to reckon with Night John. How the wise old redskin knew of the plot remains a mystery to this day. I suppose Nachte Jan got around a bit, and he had the uncanny stealth of all Indians, that faculty for making himself invisible, for hearing what he was not meant to hear, and seeing what he was not meant to see, and vanishing on unseen feet.

Anyhow, he crept furtively up to the Persen house one night in August, 1780. The family was in bed, but the Indian's light tap on the window roused Cornelis Persen. He rose and went to the open window. Nachte Jan put one finger against his lips to enjoin silence. With the fingers of the other hand he beckoned. Persen hastily donned some clothes and followed the red man. With signs and whispered words Night John made it clear to the patriot that he was in deadly danger. Hastily, Persen yoked up the oxen, first stopping to tell his wife to get herself and the children ready, and to put together all the food they could carry with them. Then, guided by old Nachte Jan, the Persen family fled to the Indian's hideout, far away amid the limestone cliffs, where they dwelt in safety until the Tory menace was past.

The White Lady

IT'S A poor kind of a family that can't conjure up at least one ghost.

My Aunt Vine is the only one who ever saw our family specter, and she couldn't identify or explain her. As far as I can find out no outstanding tragedy ever occurred in our clan. Oh, the common tragedies of death and disillusionment, discouragement and defeat, the kind that come to all, but nothing startling that I can learn. But, perhaps I do not know all.

My father was one of a large family. In the first half of the nineteenth century families had to be large because of the high death rate among infants and children. There were eight boys and five girls, all of whom grew to manhood and womanhood except one boy. My father's favorite sister was Aunt Vine. Her name was Lavina, or Wyntje, as the Low Dutch called it. All their lives they were very dear to one another. My father named one of his daughters for her.

Aunt Vine loved to write poetry and fanciful tales. In those days farm girls had to work hard. Therefore, the only time she had to write was late at night, long after the rest of the family had gone to bed. Sitting in her little room under the eaves, she would write by the light of the wavering flame of her tallow dip, or coal-oil lamp.

One night while busily at work, she heard a slight sound in the hallway outside her closed door. Thinking it might be her brothers preparing to play one of their numerous tricks on her, she rose swiftly and silently and swung the door wide open. To the young writer's astonishment the hallway was black and quiet. Aunt Vine closed her door sheepishly, thinking she must have been deceived by some noise outside her window. The next night she was startled in the same way.

My aunt was not timid. She made up her mind to find out who the midnight visitor might be. The next night she left her door slightly ajar and prepared to watch and wait while apparently absorbed in her writing. The time dragged. Shortly after the old kitchen clock had solemnly bonged out the twelve strokes of midnight, she heard a slight noise in the hall. It resembled a rustle like that made by stiff paper or heavy silk being dragged over the floor. Quickly, Aunt Vine pinched out her candle flame and peered into the hallway, which was flooded with moonlight.

At the farther end of the long hall stood a tall, slim woman, garbed in stiff-white silk, its many folds and flounces draped over the modish hoops of the day. She was gazing down the corridor directly into Lavina Hommell's startled eyes. Then, while Aunt Vine stared, frozen with fear, the apparition opened the door and vanished seemingly without sound or motion, down the precipitous, corkscrew stairway, the narrow door of which opened beside the fireplace in the dining room below.

Many a night after that my aunt would hear the stiff silk rustle and see the slender figure disappearing into the doorway that opened onto the winding staircase. She never proffered an explanation for the presence of the tall, white-garbed woman, for she had none. The lovely girl, brown curls lying against the gleaming column of her white throat, was an absolute stranger to Lavina. It was nobody she had ever seen—of that she was certain. Always the vision silently opened the staircase door and disappeared without a sound down the steep winding flight of steps, and the narrow door closed against her elaborate silken ruffles just as noiselessly.

Her brother teased my aunt about the "white woman." They said that Vine was getting queer, that she was "seeing things." The boys' jibes worried and embarrassed her and gradually she ceased to talk about her midnight visitor, but often she thought of the mystery of the lovely lady and wondered what it could mean.

The years went by. Aunt Vine's lover came a-wooing, and in time she married and left the old home. Later her parents died. The family had long since separated and gone their various ways, so the place was sold.

Then, after the passage of many years, the youngest boy, having prospered and grown rich in this world's goods, bought back the old home. Once again it was Laurel Cottage on Hommell's Hill. In his zeal to restore his childhood home Charles Hommell made over and "improved" the old house. One of his "improvements" was to tear out the winding stairway.

And never more has the White Lady been seen! Either her nocturnal visits had been so disturbed that the rustle of her silken skirts was silenced, or perhaps twentieth century eyes are "holden" that they may not see a ghost of the sixties. Suffice it to say, she comes no more.

Benedict Arnold's Wife

THE WORLD knows what Benedict Arnold did, but it will never know whether his wife was his accomplice or his victim. Margaret Shippen Arnold was a Philadelphia girl whose friends, and some relatives, were Loyalists. Others of her people fought in the Continental Army. She was a friend of the Kiersteds of Saugerties, staunch patriots. She often visited at Kiersted House, and local tradition has it that she met Arnold there while he was a brilliant leader in the American Army, and a trusted friend of General Washington.

Dr. Christopher Kiersted, the first man to practice medicine in Saugerties, was the great, great-grandson of Dr. Hans Kiersted, one of the first physicians in New Amsterdam. His sturdy stone dwelling still stands on Main Street, occupied until recently by one of his descendants—Mrs. Saidee Kiersted Ehrgott. It was in this lovely colonial home that tradition tells us that Benedict Arnold wooed Peggy Shippen. Both, it seems, were friends of the Kiersteds. Perhaps Peggy knew them through her uncle, who was a doctor, he perhaps being on terms of intimacy with Christopher Kiersted. That, of course, is only surmise. Dr. Kiersted was an ardent patriot, and it is thought that Arnold visited Kiersted House on business which concerned the Continental Army.

However that may be, the following account is the author's delineation of the courtship of that ill-starred pair. I have tried to tell this story with historical accuracy; dates, places, names, events, etc. Where no historical record could be obtained I have had to resort to imagination to help me out. I do not maintain either the truth or the untruth of my characterization of Peggy Shippen. I have merely made her into the kind of person, that to my way of thinking, would make the most interesting story.

The warm sun of a golden afternoon in late August, 1778, slanted down upon Kiersted House: Its bright rays splashed pools of brighter green upon the shaded lawn, and turned to purest gold the brown, bent head of the girl who was working busily with Mrs. Kiersted beside the back door of the house that, even in that long-gone day, had weathered the seasons of over half a century. The doctor's wife and her young friend, Margaret Shippen, were sitting on the stone-flagged back porch winding clean white rags into rolls of bandages, when both women were surprised and flurried by the arrival of a distinguished guest. They had been working in silence for several minutes when the clop, clop, clop, of a horse's hoofs was heard on the gravelled drive. The big, handsome bay stallion's rider, a cynical-looking man, clad faultlessly in the uniform of the Continental Army, appeared suddenly beside the porch.

"Good day to you, Madam Kiersted," said Arnold, gracefully dismounting from his horse and throwing the reins to the groom, who had ridden up noiselessly behind him.

Madam Kiersted arose in such haste that she tumbled the rolls of bandages across the flags of the porch.

"How do you do, General?" she stammered. "Do you bring good news or ill?"

"Neither," said the General, indifferently. " 'S-death, but I'm weary."

"Can I get you some mulled blackberry wine, General Arnold? But, first let me present my very dear friend, Mistress Margaret Shippen."

Mistress Shippen made a deep curtsey, and Madam Kiersted disappeared through the wide kitchen doorway in quest of the mulled wine.

A look of such bold admiration leaped into Arnold's dark eyes that Mistress Shippen's fair face was flooded with deep crimson. She lowered her dark blue eyes and nervously smoothed the spotless kerchief at her throat.

"Fair Margaret," he murmured, "forgive me. I'm afraid

I've offended you with my effrontery." He bent and touched his lips lightly to her small hand.

Margaret flushed a still deeper crimson, but she did not try to withdraw her hand when Arnold retained it in his close, firm grip.

The return of Madam Kiersted, at this moment, broke the tableau. The General and Margaret drew apart. Madam served the wine and the three sat talking through the soft, sweet summer afternoon. Later the Doctor returned from his rounds, removed the saddlebags from his weary, dusty horse and made himself presentable for dinner.

Arnold did not speak directly to Margaret again during the course of the evening, but often his dark, arrogant eyes sought hers; his held a compelling power. Margaret felt frightened and helpless, yet oddly drawn to this strange man. He fascinated her and, at the same time, she was repelled as if something within her was trying to warn her. "Don't trust him. There is something evil about this famous General."

Arnold stayed a few days with the Kiersteds, and every day Margaret felt more and more irresistibly drawn within the spell of his personality. When, on the day of his departure, he asked her to be his wife, she said yes like a person in a trance.

The General rode off to meet his men at Albany. The short, bright autumn days slipped by while Margaret tarried with her friends in Saugerties.

The fall and winter passed, and one day in April General Arnold drove up to Kiersted House in his great coach with the coat of arms blazoned on the doors, the coachman on the box, and the footmen behind. There were few, if any, of Washington's generals who made such show of pomp as did Arnold. Most of them were plain, ordinary men who despised anything which looked like "showing off." Not so Arnold. He gloried in anything that savored of power.

Madam Kiersted and her young guest had not expected

him so soon and there was racing and bustling in Kiersted House.

Then Margaret and her bridegroom-to-be rode away while Leah Kiersted and the doctor watched from the porch. When the great coach had rounded the curve of the drive and the fluttering farewell of Margaret's handkerchief could no longer be seen, Leah turned and threw herself into her husband's arms.

"Oh, Christopher," she sobbed, "I could not stop it. I could not stop it. But some great sorrow is coming to her as sure as my name is Leah Kiersted. This time Arnold was worse than ever I've seen him. He was moody and restless. And those strange, glittering eyes of his were never still, always darting hither and yon. He never looks at a body. What can Peggy see in him?"

Meanwhile, Margaret and the General were borne swiftly along by the spirited horses. After traveling several miles they rested and ate. Later in the afternoon they stopped in a small town where the local dominie joined them in wedlock. It was a strange marriage. The bride was quiet and almost indifferent. The groom was restless and abstracted, his bright dark eyes glancing uneasily about the room. After the ceremony the dominie shook hands, and his wife wished them well. Then they were off, the sweating horses straining to pull the heavy vehicle at the speed that Arnold demanded.

* * *

"Must you go out tonight, Benedict?" asked Margaret. The sixteen months which had elapsed since their marriage had not brought happiness to either of them. Arnold was always moody and secretive, and Margaret, still under the strange power of the man, was unhappy and frightened.

"Yes," he said shortly. Then, suddenly, for no accountable reason at all, he grew expansive. "Better times are coming for us, my dear," he said almost fondly. "I have a splendid project in mind, which, tonight I think, will see well started on its way. If it succeeds, you and I will leave this squalid hovel, these dreary barracks, go to old England to live for the rest of our days. There we shall live in comfort and luxury that I could never provide for you in this miserable, upstart country, governed by small-minded, scheming men, stupid boors who cannot recognize ability when they see it right under their noses. Would you like to live in England, my sweet?"

Margaret raised startled, horrified eyes. She stared at her husband as if he were demented. "Why, Benedict," she whispered, "what a perfectly horrible thing to say! You sound like a traitor."

For one instant an insane light leaped into Arnold's crafty eyes. He seized her arm with a grip of steel and thrust his face against hers. "Be careful what you say, woman," he whispered softly. The very softness of his whisper stifled the scream which had risen to Margaret's lips. She cringed, fully expecting a blow, although Arnold had never struck her. "Traitors hang, my love, don't forget that! But Benedict Arnold will never hang."

He dropped her arm with such suddenness as to almost unbalance her, and, turning on his heel, he strode from the room. The scales, at that moment, seemed to fall from Margaret Arnold's eyes. No longer was she under the malignant spell of the man she had married. She saw Benedict Arnold for what he was—bold, scheming, unscrupulous! A terrible battle raged in her heart. She recalled to mind her father, dying at the battle of Brandywine; she thought of her beloved cousin, dear to her as a brother, perishing of starvation and exposure at Valley Forge. The blood of these men ran in her veins. She must choose between her husband and her country.

She remembered now with terrible clarity the fact that many strange men had been coming to the fort lately to see Benedict. One night she had seen a man in a strange, scarlet uniform, mount his horse and ride away quietly, very quietly, and not in the direction of the gate of the fort. It had been a night when she could not sleep for the pain in her head. She had stood at the window and watched. There had been a man at the horse's head, leading him. The two men and the horse had melted away into the murky darkness of the night, down back of the buildings inside the fort to the westward. At the time Margaret had been in such pain, and so many people had been coming and going at the fort that she had thought nothing of it. Now, at last, it was all terrifyingly clear to her. Benedict had sought the West Point post merely for the purpose of turning it over to the enemy!

Frantically, Margaret Arnold revolved these things in her mind. Should she denounce her husband? She could not! She knew he loved her, and, worse than that, she knew that she, too, loved him with a strange and terrible intensity. She had borne him a child, and the bond between them was such that, good or evil, famous or notorious, she would defend him from the world from this time and forevermore. She could not even take her child and flee up to Saugerties to the haven of Leah Kiersted's arms. Those patriots in Kiersted House would have naught to do with a traitress. As such she knew herself to be. Yet, Arnold was her husband for better or for worse. Yes, her place was by his side. So the desperate woman reasoned.

She acted quickly, resolutely, and as calmly as if she had planned it all long before. She knew from the way her husband had spoken that whatever was going to happen would happen very soon. So she made her plans accordingly. Going swiftly into her bedroom, Margaret packed a bag with everything that would be needed for her husband, herself, and the baby for a few days. Then she stationed herself at the casement to wait.

After two hours of agonizing suspense, the dark figure of a horse and rider could be seen, threading its way carefully, noiselessly, up the river path toward the fort. So quietly did the horse and rider approach the fort that Margaret thought that nobody could be aware of the midnight visitor. However, a form stepped out from a doorway at the main entrance of the fort as the rider slid wearily to the ground. A few whispered words were exchanged, and a packet of papers was handed over to the man who had dismounted. Just then the moon came out from behind a great bank of clouds. The man who had handed over the package was her husband, Benedict Arnold. She heard the whispered words: "I dare not bring you into the fort. Conceal the small sheet safely. You may be waylaid."

Then the dark figure was on horseback again, and the animal wheeled and made off as silently as he had come. Arnold stood watching until the gloom had swallowed the horse and rider. Margaret thought dully: "Bad luck to watch anyone out of sight." But all was bad luck whichever way one looked. One swift dart of hope flashed through her mind: "Maybe he'll be intercepted. Maybe the plans of the fort will never reach the British. But what will they do to Benedict?" She dropped her face into her hands and groaned in agony.

As if Arnold had heard her, he looked up sharply and suddenly toward the apparently shuttered casement. Then he walked slowly back into the fort and in a few moments he was in the room with her. Margaret had had the presence of mind to get quickly into bed before he came, and when he entered she was successfully feigning sleep.

But the next morning the storm broke. Word came to the fort that Major Andre had been captured, and upon his person had been found the plan of the fort, which he calmly confessed he had been carrying into the British lines. From whom he had gotten these plans it was not yet clear.

Meanwhile Benedict Arnold had made his escape. He fled alone, but later he sent for his wife and the child. And, as all the world knows, poor Andre paid for Arnold's crime.

Through the many long years of exile in England, Margaret Arnold never tried to contact her Saugerties friend. Leah Kiersted died without knowing whether, in her heart,

Peggy had been loyal to her country, or whether, she with her husband, had schemed to betray it into the hands of the enemy.

The Stone in the Wall

IN 1826 a man named Markland built a "modern" hotel in Saugerties. As far as anybody knows it was he who named it the Phoenix Hotel. For the last half century of its flourishing existence the well-known inn was known as the Maxwell House. When it was razed in 1945, a man named Stewart made the lowest bid to take it down, and during the spring and summer of that year he was busy pulling down the walls, and dismantling the interior. Late in the summer, when the job was almost finished, Mr. Stewart uncovered a big semi-precious stone imbedded in the masonry. The stone was beautifully cut and resembled in size and shape a small Brazil nut. A curious, antique setting was the strangest part of the strange jewel. Two rusted and time-blackened dolphins clasped the stone, and a few inches of rusted chain still adhered to the setting. Mr. Stewart had the jewel cleaned and appraised. It was a sapphire. The jeweler thought that the stone and its setting would be about 250 years old, and worth approximately five hundred dollars. When dropped into the masonry it had undoubtedly been a man's watch charm in common use in the early part of the nineteenth century; but it must have been nearly 150 years old when it found a resting place among the bricks of the old hostelry.

Erastus Markland was a cynical, embittered man in his early fifties when he came to Saugerties in 1825. He had inherited considerable wealth from his father, a lumber dealer in Bennington, Vermont. After the death of the senior Markland, Erastus started out on his own. With great success he built and managed hotels in several small communities of New England and New York. In 1816, he had been an eligible bachelor—then in business in White Plains, New York. There he had met and married Sarah Biddeford. After one year of almost idyllic happiness, his young wife had been swiftly stricken with the dreaded "lung disease." She lingered a few months, wasting daily before the eyes of her frantic husband. In vain, he sought in New York City for some doctor who could cure her. Early in the year 1818, he watched all that was mortal of Sarah Markland placed in a grave in a small isolated family cemetery in White Plains.

In the years that followed, Erastus Markland lived to make money; he cared not how he accumulated it or what he did with it. In 1825 he went to Saugerties, taking one treasure that he prized above all else—a sapphire that had always hung at his wife's white throat. At her death, he had it attached to his watch chain. She had told him once that it had belonged to a great-aunt of her mother's and that her mother had told her that it was supposed to bring both great good and great evil to all who wore it. But Sarah had said firmly that it had brought her only good, because she was so happy in the love of her idolized husband.

One day while watching the erection of his hotel in Saugerties, walking about among the workmen, Erastus had not noticed that his "love stone" had fallen from his watch chain. That night, when on retiring, he took his great gold watch from his pocket, he saw instantly that his charm was gone. Fruitlessly he searched everywhere.

Never again did he see the one reminder of his dead wife—the charm that he had cherished all the long years since her passing.

After his loss Markland seemed to change suddenly. From a taciturn, quietly-bitter man, he seemed, in the twinkling of an eye, to become almost wildly jovial. With the opening of his new hotel, he took on the character of a more than merry host. Long after the last patron had departed, he could be found in the barroom, still drinking. That reckless conduct went on for a period of five years or more.

Then abruptly, Erastus Markland disappeared. When the help about the hotel had been unpaid for over two months, a systematic search was begun. It was many months before any trace of him could be found. Finally, through the help of a New York law firm which had handled his business for many years, it was brought to light that Erastus Markland had shot himself in a squalid tenement room on the waterfront in New Orleans. The same search brought to light the fact that he had died in dire poverty. Somehow, over a period of five years, he had managed to squander what in those days had amounted to a substantial fortune. He had caroused wildly and recklessly gambled away every last penny. His body lay in a pauper's grave in a slum section of the Crescent City. His hotel in Saugerties was found to be heavily mortgaged. It was sold to pay, in part, some of his huge debts.

So ends the sad story of a life that might have been so different. The mysterious sapphire had brought its great good and its great evil. Its mission had been accomplished, and for over a century it had lain buried in the walls of the edifice that Markland had raised. Nobody may know its history from henceforth.

"A Voice in the Darkness"

IN MEMORY OF SYBIL LUDINGTON WIFE OF EDMOND OGDEN WHO DIED FEBRUARY 26, 1839. AGE 77 YEARS, 10 MONTHS AND 13 DAYS

SUCH IS the epitaph on the only monument to Sybil Ludington, New York's female Paul Revere, the woman beloved by the Low Dutchers and all the folk of the Hudson River counties; the intrepid girl who thundered through the midnight wilderness on her father's big horse to cry: "To arms

—the British are coming!" Except that no such melodramatic summons has ever been ascribed to Sybil. The sixteen-year-old country girl, traveling alone through the darkness, simply rode to each lonely farm and crossroads tavern, slid off black Prince and knocked. "Get up—Pa says to come right away. The British have burned Danbury and there's going to be a fight."

It was the evening of April 25, 1777. In Carmel, Dutchess County, New York, some forty miles east of Danbury, the miller, Colonel Henry Ludington, had stacked the last of the sacks of flour and was preparing to close up the mill for the night. His helper had already gone home to supper and bed. Ludington was tired. The day had been a busy one, and then he was no longer young. The war years had told on him. The bullet in his left shoulder throbbed whenever the dampness of evening closed down over the valley; that bullet he had got 'way back in '54, when he went up north to stop the Indians and the French. And he would carry it with him to his grave. Colonel Ludington sighed. So much to do. He should get the men together by tomorrow night —Saturday at the latest. Somehow he felt uneasy. It was too quiet—had been too quiet for weeks—so trouble was brewing and it was well to have the men drilled and ready. Yes—he would get the troops together by Saturday. The Post was due tomorrow and the Post would take the word.

The sound of pounding hoofs, the hoofs of a weary horse, ridden to the direst limit of his speed, broke in upon the miller's reverie. Colonel Ludington shaded his eyes against the last rays of the setting sun and gazed down the road. A horse was galloping heavily up the pike, his rider lying in a strangely inert fashion almost upon the animal's neck. Something was wrong! Ludington ran to meet the horse, which had turned into the mill path. He grasped the bridle and the rider slid to the ground. The man crouched strangely against the horse's heaving side. "Are ye hurt, friend?"

"Damn British put a bullet in me. Got me as I was gettin' away. They landed at Compo Beach and they've burned Danbury. Got the stores. We gotta have help." The man slid senseless to the ground.

The miller stood gazing stupidly at the unconscious rider. What should he do? He must assemble the men. But he couldn't ride to call them and be there at the mill to organize too. Who could ride? He racked his brain. Who knew each isolated outpost? Who knew the wood paths and lonely country roads well enough to get all the men together by morning? And they must be ready then, and they would be, with himself at the mill to direct them. But he must have a rider.

A hand touched his arm. "What's the matter, Pa? Where did he come from? What happened? Shall I get Ma?"

The miller roused. Sybil stood beside him—a little girl with two, long, brown braids swinging over her shoulders. Her blue eyes were worried and as she spoke she rolled her thin little hands in her apron—a sure sign that she was frightened.

The Colonel patted her arm. "He comes from Danbury, lass. The British are burning the place—I've got to get the men together somehow and start over there. Yes, get your mother."

With the help of his wife and Sybil, the Colonel got the man into the mill and stretched on a cot. While they were busy, he told his wife the story the man had told, and also of his own predicament. How to rouse the militia and stay at the mill to organize and start them off?

"I'll go, Pa. I know the roads and I'll ride Prince. He knows them too. I'll be all right. Let me, please."

Sybil's imploring eyes looked into those of her startled parents. "You don't need to worry. I'll put on a pair of your pants and an old hat and I know where they all live—from here right straight on down to McKiel's Corners. I'll circle 'round back to get in all the farms—go over the Pawling Road and then come out by Smith Corners and down to Riddle's farm and up the Post Road." Sybil was off toward the house like a shot before the bewildered man and woman could answer.

"No, Henry, no, she can't go. The cowboys and skinners are all through the woods over there. I'd rather see her dead on the floor here in front of us."

Mary Ludington mechanically went on with her ministrations to the wounded messenger, but her face was whiter than the flour in the sacks behind them. "She will be raped and killed. We send her to worse than death. No, no—Henry, no!"

Ludington's face was a tortured mask. His country or his daughter? His lips tightened. He would never sacrifice Sybil. He would ride himself and trust somehow that the men would get themselves in shape to march.

But he had reckoned without Sybil. While he and his wife had been tending the injured man, Sybil had calmly taken things into her own, capable hands. As Ludington straightened up from his exploratory examination of the man's wounds a sound fell on his ears. A horse neighed loudly. Black Prince—the young farm horse he had purchased the past fall—stood in the barnyard saddled with Ludington's old saddle and Sybil was tightening the girth and adjusting it swiftly. Before her surprised father and mother could do more than gasp she had scrambled upon Prince's back. With a reassuring wave of the hand she trotted the horse down the mill path to the road.

"Sybil, come back. Don't go!" screamed Mary Ludington, but her voice fell on deaf ears. Prince was cantering down the road and out of sight around the first curve. The Ludingtons stood helpless beside their unexpected guest in the balmy light of the early spring evening. Their girl had gone to join the Immortals, if they had only known it.

Meanwhile, black Prince showed Sybil what he could do. He was young and fresh. For three days he had stood in the stable, for the mill and vegetable garden had claimed Ludington's attention for the best part of the past week and Prince had had nothing to do. Now he was as eager to be away as Sybil. He was a farm horse primarily, but there was speed in his long heavy strides and, as he fled away into the rose-hued evening, Sybil felt that somehow they would make the rounds. Quickly she reviewed her itinerary. She must turn to the left at Haight's farm and keep on to the east until she had covered the Putnam county settlements. Then she must work southwest until she reached the river again and come back up to this point. A long ride—forty or fifty miles, she guessed. It would take all night. Prince must not tire too early. She pulled him down to a more leisurely trot and settled herself firmly and easily into the old saddle. Good she had thought of Pa's pants and the old hat. The skinners wouldn't stop a boy dressed in farm clothes. They would think he was on an errand to a neighbor, or out to see his girl. Sybil giggled, but, child that she was, she knew the horrible danger should the skinners stop her. They must not do that. She would let Prince take it easy in the villages and settled areas and then he must go his fastest through the woods and over lonely swampland, down strange roads unpeopled and alone.

And so the big, black stallion thundered on through the night, carrying a girl with a message—a message that all the nation must hear. A summons to fight against oppression—a fight to the finish.

All went well until Sybil had ridden to her southernmost point near the river and had turned, taking a short cut through the woods to the Post Road. She was breathing a long sigh of relief, a shaking sigh welling up from her heart. Once on the Post Road she was safe! Just a few minutes more! "Hurry, Princey—I know you're terrible tired, but it's so dratted lonely through here. I hope this is the right path. I think it is. The direction is right."

A dark figure in the road ahead—a man standing squarely in the path. Sybil's pounding heart seemed to shake her body. It was too late to turn—she couldn't. She must ride him down. Prince's big frame quivered under her—he was scared. She struck him sharply with the switch she carried. He leaped at the dark figure with every muscle in his body tensed. The man screeched in fear and jumped aside just as the black stallion's great shoulders loomed above him. What he wanted —whether he was friend or foe Sybil never knew. She and Prince were around the next curve and out on the Post Road —headed for home.

It was gray dawn when the mill came into view. Prince had slowed to a walk—his black sides heaving. Men were marching in the distance—many men. Sounds of voices, orders quick and sharp—her father's voice! Men all around her now—making way for her—somebody cheering—and then more voices cheering. "Hurray for Sybil Ludington—Hurray for the Colonel's girl. Hurray—Hurray—Hurray!"

"Oh, Pa, they're here. I told them. I told them all. I thought I'd never get back—a skinner tried to stop us, but Prince pushed him out of the road."

Sybil was weeping wildly in her father's arms. Somebody was patting Prince. The men were still cheering in the semi-darkness. The awful night was over. Her ride had made the American victory sure. Ludington's militia joined the men of Generals Sullivan, Worster, and Benedict Arnold. Together they fell upon the British at Ridgefield and gave them such a beating that their retreat became a rout equal to that of Lexington and Concord.

And what of Sybil? She married her childhood sweetheart, Edmond Ogden. She gave him four sons and two daughters. Two of her sons became officers in the United States Army. One of them founded Fort Riley, Kansas. A monument is erected there to his memory. But there's no monument to Sybil, except the simple headstone in the old cemetery at Paterson, New York.

But always, as Paul Revere rides through the calm New England countryside, whenever danger threatens these United States of America—"a voice in the darkness, a knock at the door—a word that shall echo forevermore"—even so does Sybil Ludington. Her rawboned farm horse goes plunging through the midnight quiet of Dutchess and "Put" Counties: "Get up! Pa says to come. There's going to be a fight."

The Story of the Little Sawyer

BARENT CORNELIUS VROEGELEN was a Dutch boy who was born near Amsterdam in 1635. His parents were poor. In those days of so-called plenty, want and suffering stalked abroad in the world, and thievery and murder meant nothing if they gained a few crusts of bread. Barent was a student in the bitter school of want. The Vroegelens were looked upon by their neighbors as being tragically destitute. Barent was the oldest of five children; and in 1650, when he was fifteen, he could not even remember one day when he had not been hungry. He was small and stunted in growth but wiry and agile. He could and did do anything to earn a few pieces of coin to keep the family from starving.

His father, Cornelius Vroegelen, was the last, miserable tag-end of a noble old Dutch family. He was a ne'er-do-well, who spent the combined earnings of the family in the local tavern. His wife was industrious but weak of body and mind. In her youth, she had been pretty; but poverty, illness, and starvation had robbed her of all claim to beauty, and hope had long since died in her heart.

One day, Cornelius came home from the tavern, jubilant. The Dutch West India Company wanted families to settle in the New World. The patroon, a rich man of the district, interested in the company and already in America, would stock a farm for him and pay the passage across the Atlantic for him family and himself.

The Vroegelens were going to be worthwhile people again. Cornelius was wildly excited. Amelia, his wife, was to pack up all their worldly belongings at once. That, in itself, was no great task, for their poor goods were scarcely worth the packing.

However, the starved, sick woman was not equal to the

task. She and the two younger children fell prey to one of the deadly diseases which often swept through the various countries in those long-ago days. Within the course of a week, the three of them lay dead. After the funerals, Barent, his two brothers, and his father went to Amsterdam with their few belongings and presented themselves to the patroon's agent; they were soon signed up for service on land in "an easterly region along the Great River" which was already beginning to be called "Hudson's River" after the noted English explorer. The ship was to sail in three days. In the intervening time, Barent and his brothers roamed the streets of Amsterdam, marveling at the sights of the great city. They met other boys and boasted proudly of the things they would see and do in the New World. They were looked upon for the first time in their lives, with envy and admiration. Barent, in spite of the dull pain in his heart, caused by the loss of his mother and sisters, was almost happy in the thought of his great new venture.

Then came the day of sailing. All were to be on board at nine in the morning. In their miserable lodgings, Cornelius roused the boys from sleep. They scampered out into the streets, their father behind them. "Run on down to the dock and get on board, boys," he shouted. "I'll be with you in a minute." Knowing their father must always "wet his whistle," be it early or late, the boys understood the reason for his delay, and obeyed his command. They ran to the wharf and dashed up the gangplank. For a while they stood gazing over the ship's rail, watching the bustle and excitement on the dock. Then it suddenly occurred to Barent that the ship was no longer riding at anchor; she was moving out into the bay. Where was their father? He had probably come aboard, unnoticed in the uproar. But the day passed, and Cornelius Vroegelen could not be found. Evidently, he had lingered just one moment too long in the filthy tavern on the wharf. His boys were sailing to America, unchaperoned, uncared for. It was Barent who sought out the captain and explained their plight.

The captain was not concerned. What difference did it make to him that one less person was sailing, so long as his passage was paid? That three young boys would be alone and friendless in a vast, savage country meant nothing at all to him.

Remember, those were cruel days, days when boys had to be men at fifteen. It was nothing to the captain, no concern of his, and so he made it plain to Barent. Barent had not been trained in the hard school of adversity for nothing, though. He was not easily frightened. He went back to his brothers and told them that he would take care of them when they arrived in Nieuw Amsterdam and that it would be fun fighting Indians and tigers and lions. But in the dark of the night his heart would quail a bit. What would he do in the strange new land to earn a bit of bread for them all to eat? Maybe the Indians would kill them all before they could get off the boat. Of his father's whereabouts he cared nothing. Cornelius Vroegelen had never been good to any of his family. He had cruelly mistreated his wife, and that, Barent (who had loved the gaunt, patient wraith who had been his mother) could never forget or forgive. In his heart, he knew he was glad to be rid of his father, and he did not doubt that his father had purposely stayed behind. A good riddance, thought Barent.

Poor Barent, his troubles had just begun. On the third day out from Amsterdam, little Pieter, his youngest brother, who had been constantly seasick, became alarmingly worse. Somehow, Barent secured the attention of the ship's surgeon, who went with the lad to the dark little cubbyhole in which the boys were quartered. There was little the surgeon could do. Pieter died before nightfall, screaming in agony. Barent stood quietly by, clasping his remaining brother's hand while they wrapped the small form in a heavy tarpaulin. Then a tall, thin man in black, holding a book, murmured some words which Barent could not understand. The tarpaulin-wrapped bundle was quickly lifted by two of the sailors and dropped over the side of the ship. Then the sails bellied out to the breeze, and the ship went on its way.

"Two left," thought Barent sadly, "two out of seven." After several weeks of discomfort and dull monotony, the boys were glad to see a flock of land birds flying about the masts. Two days later, land was sighted, the island of Manhattan, which Pieter Minuit had bought a few years before from the Indians and was now the property of the Netherlands.

Up until then, in spite of constant thinking, Barent had had no idea what his brother and he would do or where they would go when they reached America. He was startled on the last evening aboard ship by a summons to the captain's quarters. Barent entered diffidently with his ragged cap in his hand. Once before he had seen those quarters when he had gone to ask the captain what was to become of his brothers and himself after his father's desertion. Then the captain had been exceedingly unconcerned almost to the point of brutality. This time his manner was quite different. He looked keenly at Barent, his short, stunted figure, his pale face.

"I've just been told, my lad," he said, "that the agent for the patroon, Van Rensselaer, awaits you at the fort when we land. He will inquire of you concerning your voyage. Any good word that you can say for me will put me deeply in your debt." He extended a gold coin, and Barent seized it with a muttered word of thanks. He was bewildered. The patroon, Van Rensselaer! Then that was the man to whom his father had sold them. He wanted to ask the captain whether he knew anything about that man, or knew where his brother and he might be going, and what the land was like; but he dared not. All his short life he had lived in fear of one thing or another, and fear overcame him once more. He bowed and left the room.

In a few short hours they landed on Manhattan Island. It was bedlam. People shouted and clapped one another on the back. There was much rushing about to unload the cargo. Strange, swarthy men, almost naked, were walking about curiously among the crowd. People went off in large groups and by two's and three's, and the two boys were left standing alone.

Suddenly a man detached himself from a group and came toward them. "What is your name?" he asked.

"Barent Cornelius Vroegelen."

"Where are your parents and your family?"

"This is my family," said Barent, pointing to his brother Hans. "The others died except Vater, and he did not come on the boat with us. He stopped at a tavern, and the boat sailed without him."

"I think the patroon can use you," said the agent. "The little fellow can stay here with the orphan boys until he's a few years older. Then he can join you."

At last Barent's stony self-control broke. "Please, good sir, can't we stay together?" he pleaded. "Hans can work hard, and I'll work harder because he will be with me."

The agent was a kind man, but his bread depended upon how well he managed the patroon's affairs.

"He can come later," he said cheerfully. "The orphans are well cared for here. The time will go fast, and you two will soon be together again. Say good-by to your brother, now, and wait here while I take him to the provost."

There was nothing else to do. Barent put his arms around his brother and kissed him, something he had never done before. Then through tear-dimmed eyes, he watched the agent lead the frail, little lad away. Never again with mortal eyes was he to behold his brother!

The agent was back again in a few minutes. He led Barent to another wharf where a small boat lay at anchor. "We might as well go aboard," he said, "for the crew will be lifting anchor before long. It takes sometimes two weeks to get to the patroon's holdings."

For several days, they sailed northward. Barent knew it by the position of the sun. The vessel in which they sailed was a poor, miserable, dirty, old hulk, and the food was almost non-existent, so small was the quantity. As wretchedly poor as Barent had been in Holland, the food he had eaten had never been so bad as this; a moldy crust and a little bit of brackish water each day were the rations. But if the food and lodgings were poor, the scenery more than made up for them. Barent, used to the flat, level land of his native country, had not known that there was so much sheer beauty anywhere in the world. On either side of the Great River, rolling green hills stretched away into the distance. The season was late spring, and the glorious green shades and tints of those lovely hills were dotted with the white of dogwood and shadblow. Far away in the distance, Barent could see the purple grandeur of taller hills—mountains, the agent explained. As the vessel approached nearer and nearer to the tall hills or mountains, they reflected all shades of every color Barent ever knew existed, and many that he hadn't known, especially at sunrise and sunset.

At last the boat dropped anchor in a little quiet bay. The land on both sides of the river, the agent explained, belonged to the patroon. Barent, together with several other people who had made the trip with him, was hustled off the boat. In parting from his brother in Nieuw Amsterdam, he had given the younger boy all their scanty supply of clothing, also the gold piece the captain had given him. However, he had kept one thing for himself. Long years before, in the days when his parents were young, Amelia had been as delicate looking as a lovely flower. Cornelius had given her a little heart-shaped gold locket. That, Barent had found among his mother's possessions, after her passing, and had slipped it quickly into his pocket, knowing that if it fell into the hands of Cornelius, it would soon be handed over to the local tavern keeper in exchange for liquor. The lonely, bereft boy felt he had a right to this one reminder of the woman he had loved with all the intensity of his quiet nature.

So, in the bustle of landing, he looked about him and fingered the locket nervously, wondering what they would do with him. He was not long kept in doubt. A stout, red-faced man, dressed rather better than any he had seen so far, accosted him.

"Are you Barent Vroegelen?" he queried.

Barent confessed rather ruefully that he was.

"Can you run a sawmill?" he asked.

"Yes, Mynheer," said Barent, although he had scarcely even heard of such a thing as a sawmill in the whole of his life.

"You are to come to the patroon's home for instructions," said the man, and Barent followed him up a steep, winding path through the woods until they emerged, finally, before a great log house standing in a clearing, with other smaller buildings grouped about it.

They took their places in line in the great hall and waited. Finally, they entered a small room in which sat the largest man Barent had ever seen. His huge bulk was clad in a rich, soft, dark suit. At his throat was a collar of beautiful Flemish lace.

"This is the boy, Mynheer," said the red-faced man. "All of the family died but two brothers, and the younger was too frail and small to be of any service."

"Well, we can use this one," said the patroon. "Can you run a sawmill, my lad?"

Once again Barent said he could, although he knew nothing of what the man spoke.

"Take him across the river," said Van Rensselaer. "You'll be pretty much by yourself except for the Indians, but they're all friendly. The land you can keep for yourself, but the furs and the wood you must send across. You look young to me, but probably you have a sweetheart, and likely you'll want to be sending for her some day. Is she down at the fort or in the old country? And what's your first name?"

"Barent, Mynheer," said the boy dully. "No, I have no sweetheart either at home or in the fort."

"Ah, well, that can be remedied in time," answered the patroon.

So Barent was rowed across the river, taken to the mill, and explained its working by the man in charge there. Then the latter went back with the man who had brought Barent over, and the boy was left alone in a vast, uncharted wilderness occupied only by Indians and the wild beasts of the forest. He had been provided with traps, a fowling piece, a hunting knife, and a change of clothing. Those, with some staple supplies of food, had made up the boat's cargo when they had come across.

Barent was no coward at heart. All types of fear had been his portion all his life, fear which the kind of life he had been forced to lead had thrust upon him. Suddenly, alone in the wilderness, he realized that he was free at last from fear. He was afraid of nothing. And he was in a great, new country. Barely in his seventeenth year, he was a landed proprietor. He, Barent Vroegelen, the despised and often pitied offspring of the worthless Cornelius, was owner of a tract of land so limitless that he, himself, did not know where its boundaries began or ended. It did not occur to Barent that he had not a shred of paper to show that he owned that land. The proprietor had said that the land was his. If only his mother could know!

The months passed. Barent was alone except when the patroon's agent came over to bring supplies and to collect the furs that Barent had dressed and dried. Occasionally, a boat from the other side came over for lumber. Barent always had a goodly supply waiting, sawed precisely as the orders from the patroon specified. Bands of friendly Indians often came to his lonely cabin. They learned to converse together in a sort of sign language, and Barent always welcomed them.

The months drew out into years. Often in the cool of the evening, on a placid summer night, Barent would climb to some nearby hill and look over his vast domain. As far as the eye could reach, all the land was his—his, Barent Vroegelen's. During the long, snow-bound winters, he would sit often before his leaping log fire and dream of the day when he would go down the Great River to the fort to get his brother, get

Hans, and bring him up here to share equally with him all his thousands of acres.

The years that went by made little change in Barent, physically. He was short and stunted and little, and the heavy work which caused him to stoop made him even shorter. Yet he was happy in his strange way; and, if his brother could have joined him, his cup would have overflowed.

Then, suddenly, one day in the late fall of 1665, tragedy struck. Barent was in the depths of the forest felling a huge tree. Somehow, he, who was always so sure and true, miscalculated. Perhaps his mind was too intent on the plans which he was formulating to bring his brother up from the fort. The tree fell with a mighty crash, pinning him beneath it.

Barent lay very quiet—he was not unconscious. On the contrary, his mind was very clear and alert. He knew that he was mortally hurt. To call for help and use what little breath there was in him would be worse than senseless. Who, in that empty wilderness, would hear his cry? Better use what few minutes there were left to think. Carefully, ignoring the tearing pain, he drew up his hand to his chest. He groped with his fingers until he found the gold heart which he wore tied 'round his neck by a string. When Barent's fingers closed over the little ornament which had been the possession of the only woman he had ever loved, the pain seemed to leave his wracked body. He guessed he wouldn't bother to think after all. He sighed and closed his eyes.

On the Hudson River, fifty miles below Albany, there's an old Dutch town. It has lovely colonial homes and quiet, tree-shaded streets. It's a mill town and also a summer resort. The tourists say, "What a quaint name! What does it mean? Saugerties!"

Three hundred years ago Barent Vroegelen owned "all the land from the Hudson River to the Catskill Mountains," and all unknowingly, he gave the village and the town its name. He was a man of mystery. According to the lore of the valley no white man ever saw him. He lived his solitary life on the banks of the stream that was named for his work—his millsite is known and marked, and the settlers in those long-gone days spoke of him as "de Zaagertje" (the Little Sawyer). Later came the English who added the possessive suffix " 's" making the word Zaagertje's.

And so the unknown Sawyer has a living monument that shall stand while the years and the centuries pass.

The following is a short listing of a few of the books available from HOPE FARM PRESS, 7321 Rt. 212 Saugerties New York 12477 For a complete catalogue or to order you may write ...or call 914-679-6809 to reach my answering machine. Naturally this is subject to availability and/or any price changes.

CODE: pp=pages H=hardcover P=paperback

BOOKSELLERS T=trade, S=short discount - min 5 mx

HOPE FARM PRESS AND BOOKSHOP

CATSKILL MOUNTAINS

_____BIG EYES

by Atkinson, Oriana. A well thought of novel of the Catskills by the wife of NY TIMES critic Brooks Atkinson 294pp P **$7.95T**

_____THE CATSKILLS

by Evers, Alf. The definitive, monumental study of the Catskill Mt. region by the areas most esteemed historian. This sets the standard for regional history. (see companion volume WOODSTOCK) B&W photos 750pp H **$39.50S**

_____THE CATSKILL MOUNTAINS and the Region Around

by Rockwell, Rev Charles. Reprint of the 1867 compilation of the scenery, legends and history of the Catskills by such literary greats as Bryant, Cooper, Irving and even the artist Thomas Cole. 351pp. H **$15.95T**

_____THE CATSKILL MOUNTAIN HOUSE

by Van Zant, Roland. 25th anniversary edition of this classic history of the most famous mountain house with a new Introduction by the author. color and b&w photos H $31.95S

_____HISTORIC CATSKILL

by Vedder,J.V.V. A reprint of the 1922 history of the town of

Catskill that includes some of the surrounding area especially the "cloves". so popular it led to her famous HISTORY OF GREENE COUNTY. This also has a new name index and some B&W photos. 105pp P **$12.95T**

____NOT ONLY OURS

by Atkinson, Oriana. Her story of finding their Greene County home "Prink Hill" and the history behind it.with B&W photos 150pp P **$7.95T**

____REMARKABLE HOWE CAVERNS STORY

by Cudmore, Dana. A comprehensive history of the exploration and development of the famous Catskill attraction--one of the country's greatest caves. 192pp H **$14.95S**

____TIN HORNS AND CALICO

by Christman, Henry. The story of the decisive episode in New York State history known as the anti-rent wars and the many years of suffering and terror spent breaking the tyranny of serfdom to establish democracy in the Albany area. 377pp P **$12.95T**

____Van Loan's CATSKILL MT. GUIDE 1879

From Big Indian to the Catskill Mt. House (including Overlook Mt. House), Hikes, train rides and sights...with all the ads, engravings and fold-out maps (3) of the original! 88pp P **$11.95**

COUNTY AND TOWN HISTORIES

____CLAVERACK, OLD AND NEW

by Webb, Franklin H.. Reprint of the 1892 sketch of this Columbia County community. many B&W photos and drawings 88pp P **$5.00T**

____DEAR OLD GREENE COUNTY

by Gallt, F.A. Reprinted 1915 historical and genealogical

account of Greene County. b&w photos 521pp P **$15.95**

____**EARLY STONE HOUSES OF ULSTER COUNTY**

by Teller, Myron S..Descriptions, photos and drawings of the architectural details of our historic Dutch houses. 20pp P **$3.00S**

____**HISTORY OF GREENE COUNTY**

by Vedder, J.V.V. Great New Reprint. A village by village history of Greene County from 1651-1800 with a 1927 update by town historians AND a NEW 25pp Index b&w photos 207pp P **$14.95T**

____**BEER'S HISTORY OF GREENE COUNTY**

by J.B.Beers. With biographical sketches of it's prominent men this reprint of the 1884 original is still worth reading. oversized with many b&w photos 462pp H **$45.00T**

____**HISTORY OF ULSTER COUNTY**

by Sylvester,N.B..The 1880 classic reprinted H **$80.00S**

____**A HISTORY OF ULSTER COUNTY UNDER DOMINION OF THE DUTCH**

by Van Buren, Augustus H.. Starts with the Indians and how they were affected by the first white settlers, then takes you through the burning of Wildwyck (Kingston) in 1663 and its bloody aftermath. Factual and well done. 146pp P **$13.95T**

____**OLDE ULSTER VOLUMN I 1905**

by Brink, Benjamin Myer.

Reprint of 1st. year [of 10 year] magazine with a variety of competent historical and genealogical articles dealing with Ulster County and its people, including many transcripts of original documents. Much of the material is available nowhere else. Vol II now at the printers. 384pp H **$29.95T**

____**OUT TO GREENVILLE and BEYOND**

by Beecher, Raymond. By the author of UNDER THREE FLAGS this is a well written history of Greenville area in its 2nd printing. 114pp P **$6.00T**

____**PICTURESQUE CATSKILLS**

by De Lisser, R. Lionel. Over 800 B&W photos and the stories, essays and legends of Greene County to accompany them. oversized 160pp P **$20.00**

____**PICTURESQUE ULSTER**

by De Lisser, R. Lionel. Does for Ulster what he did for Greene County with over 100 more pages! Latest printing THE BEST EVER of this nearly 100 year old classic P **$22.50T**

____**VANISHING VILLAGE**

by Rose, Will. The turn-of-the-century life of an American Village (Woodstock NY) when days of dusty roads, diversified farming and secluded country living were gradually supplanted by chaos as "artists and city-slickers" discovered its charms. FUN! 350pp H $10.00S

____WINDHAM

by Wiles, Richard C.. History of the town of Windham, Greene Co. reprinted from the Hudson Valley Regional Review, March 1985. 20pp pamphlet with map and bibliography. P **$3.50T**

____**WOODSTOCK** History of an American Town

by Evers, Alf. This colorful landmark of American regional history is a must for everyone interested in the area after reading his other tome THE CATSKILLS B&W photos 750pp H **$39.50S**

HUDSON RIVER

____**HISTORIC HOUSES OF THE HUDSON VALLEY**

by Eberlein and Hubbard. Oversized Dover reprint of this 1942 beauty. Over 200 B&W photos with histories and descriptions of

123 buildings on both sides of the river. full index, maps 208pp P **$14.95S**

_____HUDSON RIVER AND CATSKILL MOUNTAINS

by Ingersol, Ernest. A reprinted 1910 guide with detailed information and 6 fold-out maps depicting the entire valley. Filled with the historic events, geologic formations and name origins of everything on both sides of the river. A must for boaters as well as regional history buffs. 245pp P **$15.95T**

_____HUDSON VALLEY TALES AND TRAILS

by Clyne, Patricia Edwards. A compilation of the regions folklore, historical footnotes, unforgetable personalities and natural wonders. Both a collection of yarns and a great guidebook. illus. 30 B&W photos 319pp H **$18.95S**

_____LIGHTHOUSES AND LEGENDS OF THE HUDSON

by Glunt, Ruth R.. New edition with details of everyday life in 9 Hudson Valley lighthouses by someone who grew up in one. 154pp. B&W photos H **$15.95S**

_____ROCK SCENERY of the HUDSON HIGHLANDS

by Wyckoff, Jerome. A geological guide to the most scenic rock formations in the nation. B&W photos or maps every page w. index 95p P **$5.95T**

_____VILLA AND COTTAGE ARCHITECTURE

by Vaux, Calvert. First published in 1857 this treasure contains 39 great designs by this seminal influence in American architecture. All were built in the Hudson Valley. includes drawings and floor plans. 348pp P **$7.95S**

MILITARY

_____AN ACCOUNT OF THE BRITISH EXPEDITION...etc

by Pratt, George W. Recounts events connected with the

burning of Kingston in 1777. 174pp P **$3.00S**

_____THE CIVIL WAR: THE TOWN OF PRATTSVILLE...etc

by Sutch, Gerald E.. Greene, Delaware and Schoharie county enlistments and how the people left behind were affected. 41pp P **$7.50T**

_____MILITARY BIBLIOGRAPHY OF THE CIVIL WAR

by Dornbusch, Charles. Classic reference invaluable to researchers and unsurpassed in its field by the founder of HOPE FARM PRESS. in 4 volumes . SET **$130.00S**

_____120th REGIMENT, NYS VOLUNTEERS

by Van Santvoord, Cornelius. 1983 reprint of Ulster and Greene County Civil War involvement. Includes complete roster and records this is THE local Civil War book! 328pp H **$20.00T**

_____SOME NOTES on the CONTINENTAL ARMY

by Wright, John W.. These "notes" are brief, penetrating, colorful and universally acclaimed by students of the Revolution. 90pp P **$8.95T**

_____SPEECH OF GENERAL GEORGE S. PATTON

His speach to the Third Army prior to the invasion in his own indomitable language. pamphlet **$2.50T**

RAILDROADS AND STEAMBOATS

_____CANAJOHARIE and CATSKILL RAILROAD

Reprint of the 1838 report of the NYS Railroad Committee reprinted 1973. 18pp P **$5.00T**

_____CATSKILL SOUVENIR

by Helmer, William. Scenes on the Line of the Ulster and Delaware Railroad--1879. An historical sketch by the man who wrote RIP VAN WINKLE RAILROAD. 25pp P **$7.50T**

____OLD STEAMBOAT DAYS ON THE HUDSON RIVER

by Buckman, David Lear.

A revised reprint of the 1907 original. Includes a short bio of Robert Fulton and a complete account of the origins, developement and demise of steamboat service on the Hudson, with over 70 illustrations and charts plus a complete index. A beautiful 4-color Currier & Ives print of the port of New York showing all the ships has been reproduced as the cover [and is available seperately for $10.00]. over 150pp P **$18.50T**

____STEAMBOATS FOR THE RONDOUT

by Ringwald, Donald.

The only one of his famous series of steamboat books still available in its original edition. When these are gone an out-of-print copy will probably sell for $45.00 or MORE! B&W photos 145p. H **$29.95S LIMITED**

____HUDSON RIVER DAYLINE

by Ringwald, Donald. Finally, a reprint of the classic steamboat history Hudson River collectors have been demanding! Bigger and better than the original. H **$45.95S**

There is often a list of out-of-print local history books available for the asking and I am happy to provide a FREE search for any I don't have. Comments on this book and/or my catalogue are welcome. You are encouraged to write me,

Richard Frisbie care of:

HOPE FARM PRESS & BOOKSHOP

7321 Route 212

Saugerties, New York 12477